WHY CHRIST IS RETURNING TO EARTH
A Study in The Book of Revelation

Keith M. Bailey

By

Keith M. Bailey

Copyright 2012 by Keith M. Bailey

Unless otherwise noted, scripture quotations are from

The King James Version of the Bible

All rights reserved.

ISBN: 1480209325

ISBN 13: 9781480209329

Library of Congress Control Number: 2012920554
CreateSpace Independent Publishing Platform
North Charleston, South Carolina

Dedication to

All who serve the living God and

wait for His Son from heaven.

Table of Contents

Acknowledgements vii
Permissions ix
Forward xi
Introduction xv

CHAPTERS

Chapter One
   The Unveiling of the Glorified Christ 1

Chapter Two
   A Prophetic History of the Church 9

Chapter Three
   From the Heavenly Perspective 23

Chapter Four
   The Beginning of the Tribulation 31

Chapter Five
   The Tribulation Saints 39

Chapter Six
   Smoke from the Bottomless Pit 45

Chapter Seven
   The Big Angel and the Little Book 53

Chapter Eight
   Israel's Place in the End-Time 57

Chapter Nine
The Beast and the False Prophet 65

Chapter Ten
Forecasts of Victory 71

Chapter Eleven
Count Down to Armageddon 77

Chapter Twelve
The Fall of Babylon 85

Chapter Thirteen
Christ's Return to Reign on Earth 93

Chapter Fourteen
Glimpses of Eternity 105

Chapter Fifteen
Prophecy for the Soul 115

APPENDICES

Appendix A
Revelation and the Kingdom 125

Appendix B
Revelation and the Rapture 131

Appendix C
Revelation and Premillenialism 137

Appendix D
Revelation and the Restoration of Israel 143

Appendix E
Revelation and Judgment 149

Bibliography 153

Index 155

Acknowledgements

The Forward to this book was written by Dr. James L. Snyder, award winning author and the compiler and editor of the popular A.W. Tozer books.

His encouragement and insights during the writing of this book have been a blessing.

Throughout the writing of the book Britta Gibson has devoted her time and skills to produce an excellent printable manuscript for "Why Christ is Returning to Earth."

The material that made up this volume came from a series of messages on the book of Revelation given by the author at the Cornerstone Dunkard Brethren Church near Covington, Ohio. The prayers and encouragement of this congregation helped so much in completing the project.

Permissions

Brief quotes taken from Jesus is Victor by Dr. A.W. Tozer with permission of WingSpread Publishers, a division of Zur, Ltd.

Sir Robert Anderson, <u>The Lord from Heaven.</u>

A.C. Gabelein, <u>The Revelation</u>, 1915, Public Domain.

Dean Alford, Greek New Testament, Vol. IV., 1874.

William Kelly, An Exposition of Isaiah, Public Domain.

George N.H. Peters, The Theocratic Kingdom, Vol. I, 1884.

Ante-Nicean Fathers, Vol. I, Published 1884, Reprint 1989.

Forward

In these days of dismal gloom and prophetic doom, it is imperative that we see the bright side of the picture. So often bogged down with the problems of our times we sometimes forget that there is a glorious and blessed resolution awaiting. For the believer it is called the Blessed Hope. What a Blessed Hope it is.

No matter how dark the days may be, the Christian does not look down but rather looks up because he has the assurance that the return of the Lord Jesus Christ is upon us. "Ye men of Galilee, why stand ye gazing up into heaven? This same Jesus, which is taken up from you into heaven, shall so come in like manner as ye have seen him go into heaven" (Acts 1:11 KJV). Apart from this truth, there would not be much to live for these days. But, praise God we have this glorious expectation.

This represents the general theme of the book before you. It is more than that. The whole focus of this book, which is the real focus of the book of Revelation, is the systematic unveiling of the Lord Jesus Christ. This theme is developed in such a way as to leave the reader fascinated with the person of Christ. Not the details of His coming, as interesting as they might be, but the wonderful truth that He, Himself, the Christ of Revelation chapter 1, is coming back for us. Everything in the book of Revelation focuses upon Jesus Christ and to comprehend and appreciate the book of Revelation this truth is imperative.

The only legitimate thing to excite today's Christian is this One who promised His disciples, "I will come again, and receive you unto myself; that where I am, there ye may be also"

(John 14:3). This promise given so long ago is the heartbeat of New Testament Christianity. We are longing for Him to return and gather us into His home.

Many Bible prophecy books on the market are so technical that by the time you read the first two or three chapters you have exhausted your perseverance and just give up. Perhaps this is why many people complain that Bible prophecy is not for them and the books of Revelation and Daniel are not interesting reading material for them. If only they knew the wondrous truth contained in Bible prophecy. It is not just a doctrine to be touted about by professional theologians; it is not something to be read only by the religious elite, rather, the return of the Lord Jesus Christ is the Blessed Hope of the church, the only hope we can have in this world.

The beauty of this book is, it is written for people who hunger and thirst for the truth of God's Word. The book will stimulate the average Christian to think about prophecy and create an attitude of anticipation.

This book reveals the heartbeat of a man who not only loves his Lord, but is looking expectantly for His soon return and desires to encourage others in the same way.

I truly believe this book will go a long way in awakening to the truth of Christ's return. The whole system of Bible prophecy will take on new meaning. Read this book, read the book of Revelation, and then glance through the news media and see that everything is beginning to come together. No need for us to be unduly alarmed about our times but rather be alerted to the condition of our times in preparation for the return of our Lord.

If I may make a suggestion, study each chapter carefully. Read with the spirit of expectancy, allowing the truths unfolded in each chapter to minister to your spirit and fuel your anticipation for the Lord's soon return. Permit the meticulous unfolding of Jesus Christ in this book to stimulate your faith in the days of His coming glory.

Open this book and begin a journey of a lifetime. A journey that will excite you as you have never been excited about the Bible prophecy and the soon return of Jesus. "Even so, come, Lord Jesus."

James. L. Snyder

Introduction

The time has come for contemporary Christians to consider the importance of this last book of the Bible. Twenty-five percent of inspired scripture is taken up with prophecy – some that has been fulfilled and much more that has yet to be fulfilled. The modern church tends to make these prophetic Scriptures non-essential. In the light of our times such an action is an absurdity.

It is for this reason so many Christians cannot come to a valid worldview. They ignore that part of inspired scripture, which is able to give perspective to the global situation in our day. The church, like the world, is looking to the secular discipline for answers and is not finding any valid answers.

The book of Revelation picks up all the threads of prophecy from Genesis to Revelation. The eternal purposes of God are traced across the ages to the end of time and space history. No other book in the world can do that.

As surely as God Almighty created the earth and the universe, He has remained in control of the creation through the fall of man and all the disasters of human history. The conclusion of time and space history and the ushering in of the eternal age has not been left to chance. In Bible prophecy, God shows His people the redemptive events that through the ultimate triumph of Christ's Second Coming will close history in the manner He has planned all along.

This book is not a critical commentary, although issues with Greek text are sometimes addressed. It is not a devotional study of Revelation. It is a serious study of revealed truth that will nurture and sustain end-time believers in their effort to wait patiently for the glorified Christ's return from heaven.

This New Testament book of Revelation is primarily the unveiling of the work of the glorified Christ at the end of the ages. The book was written to be read and understood by all believers because it has a message for all the believers. The real hope for those who live on the edge of the end of time is to be found in Revelation.

Instead of viewing the world as the evolutionists do as a worn out planet, over populated and headed for disaster, Revelation brings into view the blessed thousand-year reign of Christ right here on earth. It will not be the fanciful utopia for which men have waited so long. It will be the kingdom of heaven on earth when the righteousness of the Lord will cover the earth as the waters cover the sea. Christ will be King of kings.

In the preamble of W.C. Stevens' book Revelation, The Crown Jewels of Prophecy, he summarizes the nature of the book of Revelation, "Something plain, not mysterious and puzzling, lies before us… it is designed to be self-evident to the servants of the Lord without distinction of class or generation… the nature of these coming events is such as to call for habitual attention and practical use of prophetic drama…" (The Christian Alliance Publishing Company in 1928, page 20).

The impact of Revelation on the believer is not speculation but sanctification. Its study is the best preparation for the rapture. Revelation calls the church back to the "blessed hope" of Christ's coming in the air for His church, a truth now forgotten by most of Christendom.

One can hardly find any area of planet earth where events are not taking place that give evidence to the approach of the end-time. The level of wars, pestilence, earthquakes, and abnormal weather disturbances among the nations is what Jesus calls the "beginning of sorrows" (Matthew 24:8).

It is time to awaken and stand alert. It is time to preach Christ to the nation like never before. It is time to purify the church. It is time to study Revelation not as a puzzle, hard to understand, but concise answers to the puzzle of our confused age. God in His eternal purposes has the situation in hand. Revelation tells us His plan for the church saints is their role as kings and priests reigning with Christ in the thousand-year reign and on into the eternal ages.

Once you understand the message of the crowned Christ to the church found in Revelation, you can never be the same. You will learn the difference between viewing life from an earthly perspective and viewing life in the light of eternity. It is the final aspects of the Lord Jesus Christ's work, which will bring the kingdom into full view.

The widespread neglect of the book of Revelation in today's church can hardly be denied. It is not being preached from many pulpits. This neglect needs to be addressed. Revelation can no longer be set aside as non-essential or just speculation. It is essential to a working knowledge of the plan of God as revealed in inspired scripture. It is relevant because it is the most complete unveiling of Jesus Christ our Lord in all His fullness to be found in the Bible.

Sir Robert Andrews, a British expositor of the scripture summed up the theme of Revelation in the following words,

> "The Revelation of Jesus Christ is the divinely given title of the book, and it governs the whole content of it. In this light, then, we read the words, 'I am the Alpha and the Omega, saith the Lord God, who is, and who was, and who is to come, the Almighty.'"

Certain it is that "The Alpha and Omega" is a title that belongs to God; and if any should doubt whether it here refers to the Lord Jesus, the fact remains that it is claimed by Him expressly in the concluding message of the book:

'I am the Alpha and Omega, the first and the last, the beginning and the end... I, Jesus, have sent mine angel to testify these things unto you for the churches."

(Sir Robert Anderson, <u>The Lord From Heaven,</u> London, Pickering and Inglis, page 93).

To have a full understanding of the offices, and powers of the eternal Christ, the book of Revelation must be studied prayerfully.

One of the devices of Satan has been to convince Christians that the content and meaning of Revelation is beyond them. This lie has kept many from feeding in the rich pastures of this blessed book. Satan knows that the book of Revelation is essential to living with victory and understanding in the dark and challenging days of the end-time.

This study of Revelation is written for the purpose of urging every Christian to rediscover the "blessed hope" of Christ coming for His church and the subsequent "coming in glory" to establish His millennial reign on earth.

These doctrines have a great bearing on how well we live for Christ and serve Him right now.

Keith M. Bailey

CHAPTER
ONE

The Unveiling of the Crowned Christ

Revelation 1

The primary subject of Revelation is given in the first verse, the Revelation of Jesus Christ. The Greek word here translated revelation literally means the unveiling of a person or object. In this blest book the veil will be lifted on the person and triumphs of our Lord Jesus Christ. He first stands unveiled in resplendent glory among His churches. The rest of the book is an unfolding of His victories over all unrighteousness, His Second Coming, His personal thousand year reign on earth and the transition into the eternal age.

The apostle John was authorized to write this portion of the word of God as the testimony of the crowned Christ. This last book on prophecy in the Bible presents the end-time in the context of the finished work of Christ. The vicarious death of Christ, His resurrection from the dead and His return to the Father in Heaven is the foundation on which God's plan for the salvation of sinners rests. That plan has a past, a present and a future. Revelation helps us see how well the future has been cared for in the finished work of Christ.

The promise in verse three is given to those who will read the book, and hear what the book has to say, and keep the truth it reveals. The promise is given in the light of the imminence of Christ's return. This gives a sense of urgency to claiming the promise.

The Salutation
Revelation 1:4-8

The grace and peace pronounced on the seven churches are from the Trinity, the eternal creator God, the Holy Spirit in all his fullness and from Jesus Christ the faithful and first begotten of the dead, the prince of the kings of the earth. After honoring Christ's many offices the focus is placed on His works as Saviour.

> "Unto him that loves us, and washed us from our sins in his own blood, and hath made us kings and priests unto God and his Father, to him be glory and dominion forever and ever. Amen."

What a wondrous picture of salvation; He loves us, He washed us, and made us kings and priests unto God. Our salvation has deeply embedded in it the clear call to serve Christ now as well as in His coming kingdom. Because this is true the book of Revelation is a relevant tool by which to prepare ourselves for the incredible future the eternal Christ has planned for us.

Then the text moves right to the focal point of prophecy: the public appearing of Jesus Christ at His Second Coming. It is the event that ends history as we know it and brings the King and the kingdom of God to earth. Christ will then reign over the nations of the earth for one thousand years.

The salutations close with a profound Christological statement. Jesus Christ openly declares Himself to be the beginning and the end. He further announces that He is eternal and Almighty. He who is both God and man is coming to earth again according to His own promises. The book of Revelation gives a broad picture of redemptive history from the first century until the end of the church age. The major part of the book predicts in considerable detail the terrible seven years known as the tribulation period that will follow the rapture of the church to heaven. Revelation is important because it is the last book of the Bible. It gathers up the threads of prophetic truth that run throughout the scripture and display their consummation in the day of the Lord. It is a bridge into the future.

God intends that the believer should come to understand the meaning of the book of Revelation and be helped to walk in holiness and in a deeper devotion to the Lord Jesus Christ. Across the centuries Christians have nurtured their souls and made themselves ready to meet Him should He come in their lifetime. It is mandatory for those who live on the edge of the end-time to make such preparation for Christ's imminent coming.

While I was a missionary among the Native Americans I came to know a native brother who was a converted alcoholic and had less than a third grade education. He lived a godly life and had become an evangelist in the tribe where we worked. I invited him to come and preach a revival meeting in our mission. The week had gone very well. The closing Sunday morning he announced that his final message would be an overview of the book of Revelation. I was somewhat apprehensive about this sermon. Later I was ashamed when I heard him give a profound message on this book. The Holy Spirit had taught him well. It was then that I came to understand anyone with a heart hungry for God and a mind yielded to the Holy Spirit could understand and be edified by the book of Revelation.

John's Vision of the Crowned Christ Revelation 1:9-18

At verse nine the aged apostle John acquaints the reader with his situation. John was the only living apostle at this time. He had been serving as the presiding elder of the church at Ephesus when a new wave of Roman persecution brought about his arrest. An island name Patmos in the Mediterranean Sea was the political prison where he was confined.

Though John was now miles from any other Christians he found a quiet place on the Lord's day and was worshipping Him in spirit and in truth. While in this state of spiritual blessing a most extraordinary thing happened to the apostle. He heard a great voice like a trumpet. The voice announced the speaker was the Alpha and Omega, the first and the last. We know that John lived with Jesus as one of his disciples for three and one half years. He saw Him after He was risen from the dead. John was present when Jesus ascended to heaven from Mount of Olives outside of Jerusalem. But John was not prepared for what he saw as he turned to see who was speaking to him. There stood the same Jesus who had lived on earth standing in all of His exaltation and glory. Jesus Christ was surrounded by golden candlesticks. The Lord had in his hands seven stars. The appearance of the glorified Christ standing before John completely overwhelmed him and he fell down as dead. Christ immediately laid his hand on the old apostle restoring his strength. Once John recovered, Christ made clear His identity as the glorified Christ.

John, now composed, was enabled to write a description of Christ's garment and His overall appearance. These details are the key to knowing this particular office Christ has taken as He stands in the midst of the churches. A look at Daniel 7:7-13 is helpful in understanding this vision. Daniel was given a vision of the "Ancient of Days" that has some obvious similarities with the vision John had of the glorified Christ. In both visions His hair is white as snow and His eyes as flames of fire. In both visions His feet are like brass and a sharp two-edged sword is in His mouth. These characteristics indicate one who judges. In this situation Christ stands in the midst of the churches as judge.

The most simple definition of the church is that given by Christ Himself, "For where two or three are gathered in my name, there am I in the midst of them." (Matthew 18:20) The New Testament church is an assembly called out of the world to be a people for His name. The Lord Jesus Christ stands in the midst of the church in His many offices, Redeemer, Saviour, Sanctifier, Healer, Shepherd, Prophet, Priest, Lord, King and Judge.

For what reason would He stand in the midst as Judge? Twice the apostle Paul wrote in his epistles that all believers would stand before the bema judgment seat of Christ to give account of the deeds done in the flesh. Such revealed truth calls for self-judgment by Christians in anticipation of that day when they stand before the judgment seat of Christ which is an experience in the future of every child of God. It is out of His heart of love Jesus takes the role of judge now as He moves in the midst of the church.

The churches are depicted as lampstands in the vision. The Greek word translated "candlestick" is better translated "lampstand" for it was a pedestal with a bowl on the top containing oil. A cloth was placed in the bowl of oil and then lighted. This symbol pictures the church as a testimony of light in a dark world. Adam Clarke once said that a lamp was worthless without oil and fire. These two elements are both types of the Holy

Spirit. When God spoke to obstinate Israel He came down on the mountain in such fire it blackened the top of the mountain. God spoke to Israel out of the fire. There is a real sense in which God still speaks in the fire. The question is have we heard what God is saying in the fire? This is a crying need of the church in the end-time. It is for that reason the Lord of the church is still standing in the midst in His office of judge. As the dark shadows of the tribulation seem already evident only the Spirit-filled church will have enough light to finish her witness before meeting the Lord Jesus in the air.

Verses seventeen and eighteen have a personal touch that ought not be overlooked. Jesus not only laid his hand on John, He said to him, "Fear not; I am the first and the last: I am he that liveth and was dead; and behold I am alive for evermore, Amen; and have the keys of hell and of death." (Rev. 1:17,18) John's body was strengthened as even more importantly his soul was freed of fear for Christ was with him all the way.

The Outline of Revelation
Revelation 1:19

The expositor of this book must be careful to let the book of Revelation tell its own story. The key to the content and order of the book was given by Christ in verse nineteen.

> "Write the things which thou hast seen, and the things which are, and the things which shall be hereafter" (Rev. 1:19).

Christ gave to John a simple outline that covers the content of the entire book. This is the key to unlocking Revelation.

My mother always kept a stone crock on the back porch of the farmhouse where I grew up. She kept an extra house key under that crock and only family members knew about it. Many years later I had made a business trip in the area of home and having completed my work decided to drive a few extra miles and visit my parents. They were gone when I arrived. The thought came to me that the key may still be under the crock on the back porch. It has been thirty years since I last looked for that door key. To my delight it was there. Our Lord kindly put a key at the door of Revelation so family members may use it to enter. The approach of this study is to lay aside all the theory of interpretation and use the key Jesus hung by the door.

John was to write first an account of the things which he had seen. This had reference to the vision John beheld of the glorified Christ in the midst of the seven golden candlesticks in His garb of judge. This takes up the entire first chapter of Revelation. Secondly he was to write the things which are. This division of the book is found in chapters two and three. It is comprised of seven letters Christ gave John to give seven congregations located in Asia Minor. These letters supply a view of the church age found nowhere else in the Bible. The Church age begins at Pentecost and continues until the rapture of the church. The church age has already lasted for two thousand years.

The Mystery of the Seven Stars
Revelation 1:20

Christ then proceeded to explain to John the mystery of the seven stars He held in His right hand. The golden candlesticks were the seven churches and the stars the angels of the seven churches. The Greek word translated "angel" in this passage can mean one sent, messenger or angel. There are no recorded incidents where angels have been assigned to local churches. It speaks of the presiding elder of the congregation who would be representative of the godly brethren called out of the assembly who are given oversight by the Holy Spirit (Acts 20:2).

These messengers are pictured as in the right hand of the Crowned Christ, the head of the church. Their position in His right hand would indicate He nurtures, guides, empowers and directs their ministry. Church leadership does well to always see themselves in the nail-scarred hand of the Lord Jesus Christ. Christ had the right to speak to His church in the first century and retains that right in the twenty-first century. He uses men, not angels, to convey His message to the modern church.

The opening chapter of Revelation establishes beyond any doubt the place of the church in end-time prophecy. The disclosure of the triumph of Christ revealed to John in the first vision on Patmos brings in the open the immediate and direct ministry of Christ to His church on earth.

CHAPTER
TWO

A Prophetic History of the Church

Revelation 2 and 3

Like no other book in the Bible, Revelation moves the heart to worship the Lord Jesus Christ. At the same time, it challenges the believer to take seriously the blessed prospect of the return of the Lord of Glory to this earth again. The two chapters of Revelation before us now are composed of seven letters Christ Himself wrote to a select group of churches in Asia Minor. The fact that only seven churches were addressed among the many already spread across Palestine, Asia Minor and Part of Europe, means this number has special significance.

The number seven in biblical numerics has usually signified completeness or the whole of something. The seven churches chosen by Christ gives a very important message to the church in every era of history.

The letters are filled with rich insights as to the nature of the early church. The churches for which Christ gave His life at Calvary are presented as they really were. The head of the church did not hesitate to speak to the weaknesses and sins of the churches. As much as He loved them, Christ pointed out their faults and exhorted them to repentance. These letters call the church to revival. Some generations have heeded the call while others have not.

The similarities of these early assemblies to the history of the church are more than coincidental. A great number of Bible scholars have concluded that Christ intended these letters to be a panoramic view of the church from the Pentecost to the Rapture. Some would conclude there was no real New Testament church since the one described in the New Testament was not perfect. Christ, who knows the hearts of these churches gave an honest view of them.

These pictures of the real church show their struggles and failures in the last two thousand years. Remember Christ is not through with His church. He will present the church to Himself without spot or wrinkle, a glorious church. What a blessed day it will be when He lifts His bride, the church, off planet Earth and meets her in the air.

The seven letters given by the head of the church are like the rest of this book: A prophecy. Coming early in this apostolic age, they portray the subsequent history of the church from Pentecost to the Rapture. Looking back over two thousand years of church history, these letters accurately prefigure the whole church age. This sacred history has blessed the church in every period of history by calling it to repentance and revival. Every true revival across the years has come when a repentant people have listened to what the Spirit says to the church.

The Church of Ephesus
Revelation 2:1-7

The church at Ephesus was a Spirit-filled, fruit-bearing congregation. They were true to the gospel given by Christ and His apostles. They had no tolerance for wickedness or heresy. They were separated from the world and preached the necessity of holiness in the life of the Christian. The Ephesian believers had been patient in suffering and faithful in their labors for Christ. But Jesus had this to say about them, "I have somewhat against Thee because thou has left thy first love." His message was delivered to them in the later days of the first century. Ephesus pictures the apostolic church from 33 A.D. until the end of the first century. The glow of the Pentecost was already wearing off. This dynamic church seemed to be very much alive and very involved in ministry, but Jesus knew their heart. They had lost their first love and unless they repented, they would lose their witness. The lesson of the first-century church is that things may look good on the outside, but the decline has set in on the inside. There seems to be a message here for the twenty-first century church.

The Church at Smyrna
Revelation 2:8-11

The assembly of Smyrna had a different experience than that at Ephesus. It was the victim of long and severe persecution. It represents the church from 100 A.D. to 316 A.D. The ten days of tribulation Jesus said would befall them took place with the ten Roman persecutions against the church during this timeframe. Christ had no condemnation for this church. He urged them not to fear the sufferings through which they were going. A crown of life was offered those who endured. Though their circumstances put them in poverty, Christ showed them to be rich in the things of the Spirit. It is the most comforting letter as the Lord of the church assures them though they may be martyred, they will not be hurt by the second death (Revelation 20:14, 15). Bright and blessed eternity lies ahead of the saints at Smyrna.

The Church at Pergamos
Revelation 2:12-17

The letter to the church in Pergamos depicts a drastic change in the church from the apostolic times. Constantine, the Roman Emperor of that time, claimed Christian conversion and ultimately made Christianity the official religion of the state. The persecution of Christians stopped, but new and alarming changes came in the church. It was never the plan of God that the church and civil government would form a union. This compromise with the secular world had devastating effects on the church. Paganism was outlawed and many pagan people were forced to receive baptism and enter the church. Many unwholesome and heretical teachings came into the church as a result of these compromises. Doctrinal changes altered the message and work of the church. The church's union with civil government often altered the truth to please the state. They lost their strong expectation of the Lord's return to set up His millennial reign. The enthusiasm for world missions declined. Many elements of the apostolic gospel were discarded.

The historic changes in the church during this period of history laid the groundwork for the formation of the Roman Catholic Church. Even during those dark days, the light of the gospel had not been put out. Jesus points out in His letter that the Antipas gave his life for the testimony of truth.

The Church at Thyatira
Revelation 2:18-29

The fourth letter was addressed to the church at Thyatira. This presents the development of the institutional church from the seventh century. The effects of the merger of the state and church continued to move the institutional church farther and farther away from the principles and simplicity of the early church. It has shifted from the message of salvation by faith to works and more works.

There was little heart religion left in this large church. Those who stood for the gospel were often driven underground. Some monks and sisters in the Roman church formed convents in which they sought for truth and found grace from the Lord. While the Roman church moved in assimilation of pagan teaching and some form of Judaism, individual Catholics sought truth and found God gracious.

The letter speaks of Christ's concern over a woman identified as Jezebel. This name is familiar to Bible readers from the Old Testament. Evidently this prominent woman became a guiding force in the church. Christ condemns the fact that the church allowed her to teach. Christ later instructed the Apostle Paul to teach, "But I suffer not a woman to teach nor to usurp authority over the man…" (1 Timothy 2:12-14). This was only one of many practices over which the head of the church was concerned. It is clear in this letter that Christ speaks to the church at Thyatira in His office as judge over His church. He showed mercy and gave time for repentance, but no repenting came to pass. Only eternity will reveal the full consequences of this great apostasy. The church of Thyatira will continue until the time of the Great Tribulation.

The Church at Sardis
Revelation 3:1-6

The letter opens with Christ's appraisal of this congregation. "'I know thy works, that thou hast a name that thou livest, and art dead." The church at Sardis portrays the church of the Reformation. Catholicism had dominated the religious scene in central Europe and North Africa and East Asia for centuries. The Waldensians and other non-Catholic assemblies were driven underground. Religious freedom did not exist during that period of history. But during the sixteenth century, God raised up men whose hearts cried out for the restoration of the gospel and the reformation of the church. A German monk by the name of Martin Luther, as he studied the book of Romans, discovered and believed the truth of justification by faith. His remarkable courage to face the system won the day and the Protestant Reformation was begun in central Europe. The Swiss reformation came about through the ministries of John Calvin and Ulric Zwingli. While the reformation was a powerful spiritual movement, its leadership adopted a policy that greatly flawed the work. They merged the new protestant churches with the state in the various countries where they were located. This move was not well received by many who had found peace and blessing in the protestant church. The resuming of the state church arrangement gave birth to a new reformation called the Anabaptist movement, from which came the Moravians, the Mennonites and the Brethren churches. They protested the church-state union and many Catholic doctrines and practices. The Anabaptist defined reformation as being a return to the simplicity of the gospel as preached by Christ and His apostles.

The question should be asked as to what aspects of this church relates to the reformation? The name Sardis has been explained as meaning something new or renewed. Another definition defines it as a remnant of those who have escaped. Either definition would fit with the circumstances of the reformation. The Sardis congregation had received the truth according to Revelation 3:3, but did not apply fully the truth they had received.

While Sardis had failure, there were those who stood true. The reformation churches are still a part of the church in the twenty-first century and will no doubt be here until the tribulation period.

The Church in Philadelphia
Revelation 3:7-13

The next period of church history is a striking contrast to the previous one. No condemnation is found in this letter. The commendation of Christ is brief, but powerful, "'...thou has kept my word and hast not denied my name." The agenda in this congregation was a message resting on the inspired scripture with everything centered in Christ. The comment in verse eight, "thou has little strength," indicates they were not dependent on numbers, money, social advantage, academic excellence, political clout, entertainment or the latest breakthrough in Madison Avenue Marketing. Like the early church, their dependence was on God alone. Philadelphia was a revival church. The years after the reformation, the churches spawned by that movement spread over the Western world as early as the eighteenth century. The spiritual fire was burning low and the church was in need of revival. A moving of the Holy Spirit began to touch England. First, the Wesleyan revival and the Whitefield revival brought a great gathering of souls. Individuals and congregations were deeply touched with spiritual renewal. The evangelical awakening spread over both sides of the Atlantic, especially in Great Britain and the United States. For most of the nineteenth century, revivals came as often as every decade. The higher life movement that swept this same geographical area deepened the concern for scriptural holiness in the churches. An important benefit of this revival was a fresh call to the evangelism of the world. A crowning feature of this awakening was a return to preaching the doctrine of the Second Coming of the Lord Jesus Christ. In verse ten, Christ extends to this church a promise related to His coming for His bride at the rapture. "'Because thou hast kept the word of my patience, I also will keep thee from the hour of temptation, which shall come upon all the world, to try them that dwell upon the earth." The temptation to which Christ refers is the Great Tribulation that is described in detail in coming chapters of this book. The revival churches have renewed the blessed hope to encourage the church to live in anticipation of Christ's coming.

The Church of Laodicea
Revelation 3:14-22

The seventh letter opens with a remarkable statement of the full deity, power and majesty of Christ, the head of the church. It is most significant in light of Jesus' words in verse twenty, which says, "Behold, I stand at the door, and knock: If any man hear my voice and open the door, I will come in to him, and will sup with him, and he with me."

The tragedy of this situation is a church that has become so apostate that the head of the church stands outside this secular, liberal, modernistic church system.

The first condemnation of Laodicea is the spiritual condition of lukewarmness. It is neither hot nor cold. The fire of the Holy Spirit has been put out by heresy, carnality and secularism. If it were cold it would at least be honest. But lukewarm is only pretense of true spirituality. Laodicea shows the level of apostasy that will characterize a large segment of the church at the end of the church age. Many of the mainline churches in the Western world today reflect the Laodicean spirit. This condition began in the late eighteen hundreds when **German higher criticism** invaded the theological schools in the United States. This low view of the scriptures soon moved many from complete trust in the scriptures, leading to the abandonment of essential Christian doctrines.

Another error in the thinking of this congregation was a total lack of faith in the supernatural. They did not live and work by faith in the promises of God. Their trust was material and secular. They thought themselves to be rich, but Jesus considered them to be in poverty from the standpoint of the kingdom and advises them to seek God through the blessings offered by the gospel. True New Testament churches can only survive by faith. As far-gone as this church was, Jesus showed them love and mercy.

Even those scholars who do not see a prophetic view of the churches in the seven letters do see the church in Laodicea as indicating decline and apostasy in the end of the church age. Paul wrote of the falling away that must occur before the day of Christ (II Thessalonians 2:3). It seems most unlikely that the prophetic scripture should show the movement in Israel and among the nations, but say nothing about the church. The church age has extended over two thousand years and impacted the world like no other movement in history. All indications are that the world is moving toward the end of the age and the glorious return of Christ. Can we detect anything in the present condition of the church that would be relevant to end-time prophecy? Are there signs in the state of contemporary church pointing to the last days? Much of the historic Christianity has sold out to the secular, the civil and the academic world. It has given in to the decadence of the day.

Christendom in the Western world is made up of Roman Catholicism, Protestant Reformation churches, Anabaptist churches, evangelical churches, the liberal/modernistic churches and the revival churches, which are portrayed by the Philadelphia church. While saints may be found here and there through all of these churches, the testimony of the lost world is very much up to the revival churches who stand for the authority of scripture, the unchanging gospel Christ gave His church in the beginning. They still seek with passion to evangelize the world. These believers seriously expect the return of Christ and the establishment of His kingdom on earth for a thousand years.

The very structure of the opening chapters of the book of Revelation shows a view of the church from the perspective of the coming of Christ at the end of the age. The omniscient Christ stood before John on the Isle of Patmos and gave a prophetic view of the entire church age. The Old Testament prophets and the eschatological passages in the New Testament provide a framework for detecting the evidences of the last day in our modern world. The escalating of political developments in the Middle East, the changes in the Western world, the weather patterns and earthquakes in our day all indicate the time of sorrows Jesus said would come in advance of the Great Tribulation. Can it not also be said that we have light on the state of the church indicating the end-time? Where is the church from the standpoint of prophecy? It is where Christ said it would be. The last four letters in chapters 2 and 3 give an accurate overview of the spiritual condition of the church in our day.

Apostasy at the End of the Church Age

We cannot leave the subject of the church age without considering what the apostles predicted regarding apostates at the close of the church age. The Laodicean church was defeated by apostasy. For the details of that apostasy one must go to the writings of the apostles.

Paul in his first letter to Timothy gave a detailed account of what would make up that apostasy in the church hear the end of the church age.

> "Now the Spirit speaketh expressly, that in the latter times some shall depart from their faith, giving heed to seducing spirits, and doctrines of demons;
>
> Speaking lies in the hypocrisy having the conscience seared with a hot iron;

Forbidding to marry, and commanding to abstain from meats, which God hath created to be received with thanksgiving of them which believe and know the truth.

For every creature of God is good, and nothing is to be refused, if it be received with thanksgiving" (I Timothy 4:1-4).

People will be led into apostasy by giving ear to false teachers who are governed by demons.

In his second letter to Timothy Paul again writes the dangerous apostasy that will attack the church in the last days. The nature of this apostasy will be different than the discontent in the First Epistle of Timothy. That apostasy is doctrinal. Satan, by false doctrine, will corrupt the church and destroy its spirit and effectiveness. The second warning speaks of apostasy that taints the behavior of professing of Christians.

"The apostle said, 'This know also, that in the last days perilous times shall come.

For men shall be lovers of their own selves, covetous, boasters, proud, blasphemous, disobedient to parents, unthankful, unholy, without natured affection, truce breakers, false accusers, incontinent, fierce, despisers of those that are good. Traitors, heady, high-minded, lovers of pleasure more lovers of God. Having a form of godliness, but denying the power thereof: from such, turn away" (2 Timothy 3:1-5).

The evening news any night in the week verifies that both forms of apostasy prophesied by the apostles has broken loose in our present culture and greatly deadens the testimony of the church.

The characteristics of the Laodicean church are clearly evident in our day indicating the end time is approaching. The apostasy prophesied by Paul is already a reality in the churches of the western world.

How Will the Church Age End?

According to the New Testament, the close of the church age will be a prophetic event associated with Christ's Second Coming. The scriptures show that Christ's return will take place in two phases. Paul described the first phase in I Thessalonians 4:16,17;

> "For the Lord Himself will descent from heaven with a shout, with voice of the archangel, and with the trump of God; and the dead in Christ will rise first:
>
> Then we which are alive and remain shall be caught up together with them in the clouds, to meet the Lord in the air: and so shall we ever be with the Lord."

This event is called the rapture of the church. The bodies of all dead Christians will be resurrected and joined with their spirits. Immediately afterwards the bodies of all living Christians will be made immortal and incorruptible on the spot and they too will join the resurrected Christians to meet the Lord in the air (I Corinthians 15:51,52).

The church age then terminates when Christ gathers all of His church to meet Him in the air. He will take them all to heaven where they will reside during the dark days of the tribulation. The second phase of Christ's Second Coming takes place seven years later at the end of the Great Tribulation. The Lord

Jesus will come out of heaven on a white horse followed by the armies of heaven (His bride, the church).

Following the outline of Revelation, Christ next gave to John the third division, the things that will be hereafter will be introduced in chapter four.

CHAPTER
THREE

From the Heavenly Perspective

Revelation 4 and 5

At the completion of the letters to the seven churches John saw a door open in heaven. A voice that sounded like a trumpet said to the aged apostle, "Come up hither and I will show you things which must be hereafter." Christ had advised John that he should write of his vision of the Glorified Christ in the midst of His churches. He was told to include the letters to the seven churches providing a helpful overview of the church age. Now John is about to be introduced to the things that must be hereafter. These next chapters will provide a prophetic preview of God's plan for the end-times and the termination of history.

Many expositors of Revelation have attempted to associate these future events with history. The result of this approach is confusion. Most of Revelation deals with the future. From chapter four to the end of the book the future is in view.

In this chapter the focus is different. John is himself in heaven and will begin to see the unfolding of prophecy from the heavenly perspective. Much of what takes place in this section of Revelation originates in heaven though it may greatly affect circumstances on the earth. That is a doctrinal truth we need to lay hold of. The close of history is more a matter of heaven than it is of earth.

Now it is time to join John in the throne room of heaven. His first impression was the wonder of God seated on His throne. The Old Testament Psalmist when he saw the moral beauty of God prayed, "Let the beauty of the Lord our God be upon us."

John saw the beauty in terms of precious stones. It is clear that everything Revelation has to say to us is anchored in the moral beauty and the perfect attributes of Almighty God. He has complete knowledge of all that has happened and all that is now transpiring and finally all that is yet to happen.

Bible prophecy is the strongest evidence that God is omniscient. Hundreds of prophecies have already been fulfilled. Just the prophecies that predicted the birth, ministry and work of Christ are sufficient to confirm the all-knowing power of God.

A Closer Look at the Throne Room
Revelation 4:4-8

Round the throne of God were twenty four seats, the Greek word is "throne." These were occupied by twenty-four elders dressed in white raiment and each with a gold crown on his head. The Greek word translated "crown" is stephanos which is not the crown of a ruler but a crown given as reward to those who won athletic events.

The same word is used in the New Testament for the rewards that will be given the faithful for dedicated service to Christ.

Thunder and lightning and voices came from the throne of God. Seven lamps of fire burned before the throne representing the seven Spirits of God. There is only one Holy Spirit therefore the seven lamps do not mean seven Holy Spirits but represent the fullness of the personality and works of the third person of the Trinity. In both the Old and the New Testaments fire is used as a type of the Holy Spirit.

John's eyes fell on the sea of glass that was like crystal and lay before the throne. Revelation 15:2 speaks of a similar sea on which people were standing and playing harps. Evidently this sea was not liquid but hard like pavement and provided an approach to the throne.

An order of angels here called beasts, best translated "living creatures," were around the throne. Careful attention should be given the features of the four "living creatures" for they are helpful in identifying them. They are described as being full of eyes before and behind. The first "living creature" looked like a lion. The second, like a calf, the third had the face of a man and the fourth was like an eagle. The prophet Ezekiel saw angels similar to these "living creatures" (Ezekiel 1:5-10). The "living creatures" are identical with the cherubim and are the guardians of the holiness of god. They never rest but day and night continue to say, "Holy, Holy, Holy, Lord God Almighty, which was, and is, and is to come." These four angelic beings seem also to call attention to the redemptive offices of the Lord Jesus Christ. The lion presents Him as king, the calf as a servant, the man as the incarnate Son of God and the eagle the symbol of Christ's deity.

The Heavenly Worship of God the Creator Revelation 4:9-11

The fourth chapter ends with a crescendo of worship by the four "living creatures" and the twenty-four elders. It begins when the "living creatures" give glory and honor and thanks to Him that sits on the throne. As the Bible opens with the account of creation so the last book of the Bible we hear angels and saints adoring Almighty God for His work of creation. God spoke to Job in the Old Testament asking if he was present when the sons of God shouted for joy. Now once again at the end of time and space history angels and saints take up this ancient hymn. The twenty-four elders were so moved they cast their golden crowns before the throne in deep adoration and worship.

The Opening of the Sealed Book
Revelation 5:1-7

This magnificent scene is continued in the fifth chapter. Attention is called to a book with seven seals held by God the Father on His throne. Immediately a strong angel was dispatched to call throughout the universe for one able to open the book and to loose its seven seals. No response came and John was so distressed he fell weeping. One of the twenty-four elders approached John and told him that the Lion of the tribe of Judah would open the book. John looked up and saw not a lion but a Lamb as it had been slain. This is the glorified Christ and He goes immediately to the throne and receives the sealed book from the Father's hands.

What is there about this book that creates such interests in the courts of heaven? The description would indicate that it is a title deed, the title deed to the created universe which was placed under a curse at the time Adam and Eve fell in sin. Paul says in Romans 8:22, "For we know that the whole creation groaneth and travaileth in pain together until now." That passage indicates the hope of a coming deliverance from this bondage. The creation so long under Satan's dark reign is about to be delivered by the Lord Jesus Christ at His Second Coming.

As Christ takes the title deed the "living creatures" and the twenty-four elders prostrated themselves before the Lamb.

They had harps and viols of odours which were the prayers of the saints. During this time of worship they sang a song that exalted the Lord Jesus Christ rejoicing that He is worthy to open the sealed book. The words of this song declare Christ worthy because he has redeemed them by His blood from every people, tribe and nation. This tells us that the twenty-four elders are not an order of angels but the raptured church now in heaven with her Lord.

This song is the key to identifying the twenty-four elders so prominent in this section of the Revelation. It is often said that the church drops out of sight from chapter four to the end of the book. It is true that the word "church" is not found from chapter four through twenty-one. But it is not true that the church is out of sight and insignificant for that time.

Let us read carefully the song of the twenty-four elders,

> "Thou art worthy to take the book, and to open the seals thereof: for thou wast slain and has redeemed us to God by thy blood out of every kindred, tongue, and people, and nation; and hast made us unto our God kings and priests: and we shall reign on the earth" (Rev. 5:9,10).

The Identification of the Twenty-Four Elders

To interpret this passage the identity of the twenty-four elders seated about the throne of God must be clear. This process can begin with noticing their clothing and their crowns. The elders were dressed in white raiment, the garb of the righteous and the overcomers (Rev. 3:5). They had gold crowns on their heads. The Greek word in this text means a reward for service. The same word is used of the rewards given to believers (II Tim. 4:8). The song of the elders clearly states they were redeemed by the blood of the Lamb. The song also indicates they wre redeemed from all the tribes and nations of the world as is the New Testament church. They sit on thrones next to the throne of God, a position reserved for those who by Christ their Lord have been made kings and priests unto God.

All of the above distinctives are used exclusively of Christians, those who by saving grace are in the body of Christ. The twenty-four elders represent the church now raptured and in heaven. The church has not dropped out of sight. It is plainly with Christ in the throne room of heaven and very much aware of the unfolding of God's dynamic plans for the close of history and the transition to eternity. Why are there twenty-four elders? It has been suggested that this number is the composite of the twelve tribes of Israel and the twelve apostles of the New Testament church and represent the raptured Old Testament saints and the church saints.

There is one other issue with the identification of the elders that should not be overlooked. In the song to the Lamb in Revelation 5:9 the King James Version says, "Thou art worthy to take the book, and to open the seals thereof, for thou wast slain and hast redeemed (us) to God by thy blood…" (Revelation 5:9, 10). The New American Standard Version says, "Worthy art thou to take the book, and break its seals, for thou wast slain and did purchase for God with thy blood (men) from every tribe…" The difference in these two versions reflects the Greek text from which the translations were made. The King James was translated from the Received Text while the New American Standard was done from the Wescott and Hort text. For most of a century it was assumed that since the Wescott and Hort manuscripts being the oldest yet discovered would be the most accurate. Time has proven that theory to be wrong. Over time flaws were discovered in the Alexandrian text found by Wescott and Hort. The Siniaticus manuscript was discovered and proved to be as old as the Alexandrian. It uses "us" in the text. It means the manuscript evidence is supportive of retaining "us" in the text. It means that the twenty-four elders identified themselves as blood bought children of God saved out of the nations of the world.

It becomes evident that the church has been raptured by this time and is present in heaven. It is also evident that their rapture to heaven took place before the tribulation began.

All Creation Joins in Adoration

As the heavenly choir exalted the Lamb the scripture says that every creature in all the universe joined the praise and began to say, "Blessing, and honor, and glory, and power be unto him that sitteth upon the throne and unto the Lamb forever and ever." The heavenly hosts fell down before the Lamb and worshipped Him. From this brief visit to heaven with John one cannot miss the fact that worship is the way of life in the throne room of glory.

CHAPTER
FOUR

The Beginning of the Tribulation

Revelation 6

Tribulation has been part of the human experience since the fall of man. But when the prophetic scripture speak about a tribulation it does not mean the usual troubles that challenge the believer. The Bible predicts numerous times an intense but short tribulation period will take place just prior to the Second Coming of Christ. Many of the Old Testament prophets warned of the coming tribulation.

Jeremiah speaking of the last days said,

> "For lo, the days come, saith the Lord, that I will bring again the captivity of my people Israel and Judah, saith the Lord: and I will cause them to return to the land that I gave their fathers, and they shall possess it."

And these are the words that the Lord spoke concerning Israel and concerning Judah:

> "For thus saith the Lord; We have heard a voice of trembling, of fear, and not of peace.
>
> Ask now and see whether a man doth travail with child? Wherefore do I see every man with his hands on his loins, as a woman in travail, and all faces are turned into paleness? Alas for the day is great, so that none is like it; it is even the time of Jacob's trouble; but he shall be saved out of it" (Jeremiah 30:3-7).

Another important prophecy relating the coming tribulation period to the restoration of Israel is Daniel 12: 1 which reads,

> "And at that time shall Michael stand up, the great prince that standeth for the children of thy people: and there shall be a time of trouble, such as never was since there was a nation even to that same time: and at that time thy people shall be delivered, every one that shall be found written in the book."

Christ in his Olivet sermon makes this powerful summary statement about the tribulation:

> "For then shall be great tribulation, such as was not since the beginning of the world to this time, no, nor ever shall be.

And except those days be shortened, there shall no flesh be saved: but for the elect's sake those days shall be shortened" (Matthew 24:21-22).

Christ's statement makes clear that the Great Tribulation is not a matter related only to Israel but a world-wide disaster affecting all mankind.

Before considering the beginning of the Tribulation there is one other Old Testament prophecy that will provide some essential details about this the most intense of all end-time prophecies. In the ninth chapter of the book of Daniel we find the prophet engaged in a prolonged prayer session. His particular burden was for the future of his people Israel.

Daniel 9:24-27

The answer was brought to him by an angel. God showed Daniel that the future of his people would be revealed by seventy prophetic weeks a total of 490 years. It begins when Artaxerxes gave orders for the repair and rebuilding of the city of Jerusalem. The scripture says this order was given in the month Nisan in the twentieth year of Artaxerxes which was 445 B.C., from the month Nisan 445 B.C. to April 6, 32 A.D. when Christ rode into Jerusalem at His triumphant entry is exactly 483 years to the day. That accounts for sixty-nine of the seventy weeks. One week remains. The seventieth week has not yet been fulfilled. Where does it fit into Bible prophecy? There is obviously a time lapse between the fulfillment of the sixty-nine weeks and the seventieth week. Daniel was told some happenings and personalities of the seventieth week.

The prince who is to come will make a covenant with Israel for a period of seven years. The prince mentioned here is the antichrist and he will break treaty with the Jews midway in the tribulation. This passage is very important in that it tells us how the tribulation will begin and how long it will last. The tribulation will continue for seven years. This fits the pattern in the book of Revelation where we find the tribulation made up of two three and one half year periods. Chapters six through nineteen cover the events of this most troubled time in human history.

The First Seal
Revelation 6:1-2

With these insights attention must be given the opening of chapter six where the tribulation is about to begin. Christ has taken from the Father's hand the title deed to the universe and is ready to open the first seal. John says of the first seal,

> "And I saw and behold a white horse: and he that sat upon him had a bow; and a crown was given unto him: and he went forth conquering and to conquer" (Revelation 6:2).

The rider of the white horse has mistakenly been thought to be Christ. Such an idea is contrary to the facts. Christ will personally return mounted on a white horse as recorded in Revelation 19:11. This will take place at the end of the Great Tribulation. The rider on this white horse in Revelation 6:2 is a cheap imitation of Christ. This rider is the antichrist. He receives his power from the newly revived Roman Empire. According to the prophecies in Daniel, a ten nation confederacy will come to power in the geographical areas of ancient Rome. At this time, the beginning of the tribulation, this governmental power will be strong enough to sustain the antichrist in his bloodless but deceptive take-over of the world government.

The Second Seal
Revelation 6:3,4

When Christ opened the second seal there came a red horse. The rider of the red horse is empowered to take peace from the earth. We assume that war will take away peace from the nations but like the contemporary world, riots and protests can devastate the economy and paralyze the political situation. Unrest and chaos will no doubt be part of the methodology employed by the rider of the red horse.

The Third Seal
Revelation 6:5,6

The third horseman rides a black horse and has in his hand a pair of balances. From the midst of the four living creatures comes a voice announcing a shortage of wheat and barley, which will cause worldwide hunger. Prices indicate the cost of these necessary commodities will be so high the ordinary working person will not be able to afford them. The instruction to hurt not the oil and the wine suggests that this totalitarian global government will protect the rich from this international famine.

The Fourth Seal
Revelation 6:7,8

As Christ opens the fourth seal a pale horse named Death comes into view. Death and hell are said to ride with this horseman. A voice says that death and hell will have power over one fourth part of the earth. The purpose of the pale horse is wholesale killing by every possible means. Death by the sword infers war. Starvation will be part of this disaster. Even wild animals will attack humans on a large scale leaving many dead. It is hard to imagine the conditions on earth by the end of the fourth seal judgment.

The Fifth Seal
Revelation 6:9-11

At the close of the fourth horsemen's deadly work, Christ opens the fifth seal. It is in vivid contrast to all the others. John saw under the altar the souls of the martyrs whose lives had been given for the testimony of the gospel of Christ. They were greatly exercised and asked when vengeance would be taken on the ungodly earth-dwellers. These are no doubt the first martyrs of the tribulation period. Many more will join this company of souls under the altar. More will be revealed about this company of saints in subsequent chapters.

The Sixth Seal
Revelation 6:12-17

The sixth seal brings an earthquake of unusual magnitude and is attended by the changes in the heavenly bodies. The sun becomes black and the moon takes on the color of blood. The earthquake will move mountains and islands from their places. The stars are said to fall like figs shaken by the wind. This mighty earthquake is not just a natural disaster but an intentional act of divine judgment on a wicked world.

One would expect that the hardest of hearts would be moved by such devastation but the kings, the great men, the rich, free men and slaves prayed not to God but to the mountains to hid them from the face of God. They are fully aware that the day of God's wrath has come and they show no inclination to repent of their sins or to yield to the Lamb.

The reaction of earth-dwellers to the seal judgments was prophesied by Christ as He was on His way to Calvary. A group of women were weeping and wailing at the awful treatment of Christ. Jesus turned to them and said, "Daughters of Jerusalem, weep not for me, but weep for yourselves, and for your children.

For behold the days are coming, in which they will say, 'Blessed are the barren, and the wombs that never bore, and paps which never suck!' Then they will begin to say to the mountains, 'Fall on us!' and to the hills, 'Cover us!' For if they do these things in the green tree, what shall be done in the dry?" (Luke 23:28-31).

Christ was speaking of the similar circumstance as will occur at the close of the sixth seal. Rather than repenting and calling for mercy the hardened earth-dweller will pray for the mountains to hide them from the judgment of Him that sitteth on the throne and from the evident wrath of the Lamb. According to Revelation 6:16 the earth-dwellers will see Christ on His throne. But their stone cold hearts will only plea for the mountain to hide them from the sight of the Lamb of God.

Knowing full well they are dealing directly with Christ who alone can save them. With hateful hearts they will reject Him and choose eternal damnation.

This passage assists in understanding the level of judgment of God will pour out on the world during the tribulation. He is completely just in doing so. Those who cry to the mountain in that awful day will have knowingly sinned away God's grace.

CHAPTER
FIVE

The Tribulation Saints

Revelation 7

The seventh chapter of Revelation is parenthetical. It breaks into the sequence of judgments with important information about God's plan for evangelism during these dark days of the tribulation. The church is no longer on earth but raptured to heaven. How then could evangelism be possible? This chapter answers that question.

John first sees four angels standing on the four corners of the earth. Their duty is to restrain the wind so it would not blow on the earth or sea, evidently to prevent any natural disaster. A very important spiritual transaction was about to take place. Coming from the east was another angel commissioned to put the seal of the living God on 144,000 Jews.

God only puts His seal upon those who are saved as Paul taught in Ephesians 1:13, "...after that we heard the word of truth the gospel of your salvation; in whom also after that ye believed, ye were sealed with that Holy Spirit of promise." This group of Jews is called the servants of God and they are sealed on their foreheads. The number 144,000 is made up of 12,000 from each of the twelve tribes of Israel. It is not until John sees the next vision that the mission of the 144,000 is made clear.

The apostle's attention was next drawn to heaven and the throne room. A multitude so great it could not be counted stood before the throne and the Lamb. They came from all the peoples, tribes and languages of the world. Heaven resounded with their praise and worship. They were joined by the angels and the twenty-four elders in thanksgiving and exaltation to God.

The contemporary church should prayerfully take heed to the love of worship reflected in the heavenly hosts. Their worship needs no methodology. The angels and the redeemed are moved to worship by a deep inner passion for God. It need not be stimulated for it is always there.

The angels and the twenty-four elders began to ask as to the identity of this multitude of saints that had recently joined them. One of the elders said, "...These are they which came out of great tribulation, and have washed their robes and made them white in the blood of the Lamb." This multitude is made up of people washed in the blood of Christ. They are saved. Is this not then the raptured church? Look more carefully at verse fourteen. It describes the multitude as coming out of great tribulation which would infer that they are people who have suffered through much tribulation. However, if this passage is examined in the Greek, one discovers the literal translation says, "they came out of the tribulation, the great one." This multitude is not the New Testament church nor is it a gathering of people who suffered tribulation in general. These are souls saved during the great tribulation, the seven year tribulation just before Christ returns.

This newly saved multitude in glory is the fruit of the blessed work of the 144,000 Jewish evangelists. In the worst years of human history the grace of God will still be reaching out to sinners. While many earth-dwellers will be hopelessly evil and turn a deaf ear to the truth there will be that minority that has never heard the truth and will receive it with joy and often at the expense of their lives. Daniel spoke of this unusual evangelism in the end-time, "and they that be wise shall shine as the brightness of the firmament; they will turn many to righteousness as the stars forever and ever" (Dan., 12:3).

The introduction of 144,000 in chapter seven establishes the critical place Israel has in the unfolding of Revelation. In the modern religious scene the so-called replacement/theology has cast a shadow over the revealed truth about Israel in the last days. This school of thought maintains that God is finished with Israel and therefore, this people and nation has no place in the unfolding of Bible prophecy. Nothing could be farther from the truth. God made unconditional promises to Abraham and He will keep every one of them.

One leaves this chapter with the shouts of joy and the adoration of the blood washed throng in heaven's throne room. No matter how dark and terrible the tribulation nightmare becomes, God will continue to carry out His prophetic purposes with perfect justice and a merciful heart. The doctrine of last things can best be kept in perspective by constant reference to the dying Lamb. In the midst of the throne room the slain Lamb stands resurrected from the dead and alive forever more. This name of Christ echoes throughout the book of Revelation. It is the name that best displays His work at the cross. All of the redemptive history and prophecy rest on the slain Lamb. It's the shed blood that makes Him worthy.

Not every Gentile saved during the tribulation will be in this multitude in heaven. All of these died for their faith. Others will escape martyrdom and will be alive when Jesus arrives on earth. They will become part of the population of the millennial earth (Matthew 25:31-40).

The 144,000 witnesses are called the servants of God confirming their spiritual credibility sealed by the seal of the living God which shows them to be the rightly related to God. This mighty seal served as protection from the antichrist and all the forces of evil. It must be assumed that many saved by their witness will be Jews and those who survive will be part of the population during the millennium. It is evident that at this point in history God still loves Israel and sees for her a blessed future.

The spiritual movement that follows the ministry of the 144,000 Jewish evangelists will exceed any revival in history past. In less than seven years such a large number will have been converted to Christ. They will represent all nationalities, people groups and languages of the world.

An ingathering of souls of this magnitude implies an outpouring of the Spirit greater than Pentecost. It will take place in the midst of difficult and threatening conditions. This great harvest will be among those who did not hear the gospel during the church age. The church is now raptured and in heaven and no longer bears the gospel witness here on earth. Newly converted Jews now take up the task of making Christ known as the only Saviour given among men whereby they may be saved.

Those who heard the gospel and rejected it will not respond to this awakening. Paul describes their situation in 2 Thessalonians 2:10-12:

> "...because they received not the love of truth, that they might be saved. And for this cause God shall send them

strong delusion, that they should believe a lie: That they might be damned who believe not the truth, but have pleasure in unrighteousness."

Those who reject Christ and are still surviving will refuse to repent and believe the gospel when preached by the Jewish witnesses. They will be easy victims of the antichrist's lie.

CHAPTER
SIX

Smoke from the Bottomless Pit

Revelation 8 and 9

The silence of God can be significant and there is also worth in the silence of His people. For four hundred years God was silent and gave not one single word of inspired scripture from the close of Malachi until the New Testament. This silence in the throne room of heaven was because of the work God was about to do. It should not be overlooked that silence can be a most hallowed act of worship. Worship is not always praise; it can be the devotion of total silence when the circumstance requires it. It must be admitted that the silence of Revelation

6 honored God as much as the vocal adoration of angels and saints.

After the tribulation saints are introduced Christ opens the seventh seal of the title deed. This action was immediately followed by one half hour of silence in heaven. The praise and singing of the heavenly host both raptured saints and angels suddenly were quiet.

The breaking of the seventh seal made possible the complete opening of the title deed of the universe making known the extent of the wrath of the Lamb yet to be released upon the earth- dwellers.

The silence was broken when seven angels stood before God and were given seven trumpets. Another angel stood before the altar and with incense offered the prayers of all the saints upon the altar. With the smoke of the incense the prayers of the saints ascended before God. The angel took the censor and filled it with fire from the altar and cast it on the earth. This action was attended by voices, thunder and lightning and earthquakes. The priestly action of this angel signaled the resumption of the judgments on earth. The impact of the prayers of the saints on fulfilled prophecy cannot be overlooked. The consideration during the silence was the power of the prayers of the saints. The angels using the censor to cast fire on the earth from the golden altar of incense adds a larger dimension to prayer. The judgment of Christ rejecters, the defeat of the powers of darkness and the bringing of the kingdom of the Lord is, to some degree, the fruit of the prayer. One of the most powerful forces in the universe is the prayers of the saints. One does not expect a lesson on prayer in a book like Revelation but it is definitely there. The second series of divine judgments are ready to begin and seven angels stand ready to sound their trumpets.

The First Trumpet

As the first angel sounded his trumpet there was showered upon the earth hail and fire mingled with blood. This disaster destroyed a third of the world's trees and all the green grass was burned. Incredible sounds of thunder, lightning and earthquakes preceded the deadly shower of hail and fire mingled with blood.

The trumpet judgments seem to follow one after another and are completed in a short time span.

The Second Trumpet

Trumpet number two was an even greater catastrophe. A mountain on fire was cast into the ocean and one third of the oceanic waters were turned to blood, one third of fish and other creatures in the ocean died. This would have a great impact on the world's food supply. At the same time, one third of the international shipping industry was wiped out. Those who dwelt on earth could not recover from one trumpet when another sounded.

The Third Trumpet

When the third angel sounded, the star fell from heaven. It was burning as a lamp and fell on a third of the rivers and other fountains of water essentially polluting a third of the world's freshwater supply. The star was called wormwood. It made the water bitter and unfit for human consumption.

The Fourth Trumpet

This judgment was directed at the sun, the moon and the stars. The third of these heavenly bodies became dark. The light from the sun so essential to life on earth will be cut off for one third of the earth's surface. The maintenance of human life becomes more and more difficult.

As the earth dwelling humans try to reckon with the damage of the first four trumpets, an angel flies through the heavens giving warning of the three woes yet to be released on the inhabitants of the world.

In the first verse of Chapter nine, the change begins in the nature and intensity of the trumpet judgments. This is one of the darkest chapters in the Bible. Here for a brief time God Almighty lifts the lid off of hell and allows it to overflow on the earth.

Before taking up the study of these three judgments, time should be given to the hermeneutics to be used. Is it to be understood symbolically or is it to be understood literally? A basic rule of interpretation is to treat the passage literally unless there is evidence in the context that calls for another hermeneutical approach.

Numerous commentaries on the book of Revelation have looked upon this ninth chapter as symbolical. They have yielded some fanciful interpretations. Efforts have been made to interpret the creatures in this chapter as depicting modern military equipment. This approach ignores the stated nature of this passage. What this chapter is really about is the ultimate spiritual warfare. The final trumpets show what the worst powers of hell can do on planet earth.

The Fifth Trumpet

When the fifth angel sounded his trumpet a star fell from heaven to earth. The fallen star is Satan himself and to him is given the key to the bottomless pit. When he opened the pit the smoke came out darkening the air and the sun. This begins the dreadful days of the three woes directed against the rebellious earth-dwellers. Satan and his demons will bring from the bottomless pit everything their wicked and warped intelligence have designed to horrify the earth population during this part of the Great Tribulation.

To the intellectual arrogance of the Western world this chapter has the appearance of a Hollywood horror movie, not to be taken seriously. But for those who know the authority of inspired Scripture the days and months described in this ninth chapter of Revelation is certain to happen. The forces of hell are going to be released and in time and space history do their worst to mankind still resident on earth.

The Opening of the Pit

As the bottomless pit is opened it will fill the atmosphere with smoke. Creatures called locusts will come in large numbers. It is obvious that they are not natural locusts but demons equipped to bring great suffering on earth. Unlike natural locus, these demonic locusts will not bring harm to plants. Scripture says they have been instructed to limit their attacks to people who do not have the seal of God on their foreheads.

The demonic locusts are not to kill people but torment them for a period of five months. Those stung by these locusts will be in such agony they will desire to die but will be unable to die. It staggers the mind to think what life on earth will be like during the five months of this trumpet judgment.

Revelation 9:7 through 10 gives a detailed description of the demonic locusts. They are weird, grotesque and terrorizing. Unlike natural locust, which has no leader, the demonic locusts are under the direction of one called in Hebrew "Abaddon" and in Greek "Apollyon." He is King of the bottomless pit. The first and worst of the fallen angels will use his accumulated wickedness to torment humans on earth that have by his lies been deceived to reject Christ.

The Sixth Trumpet

Now the fifth trumpet woe is over and John is reminded of the more woes just ahead. As the sixth trumpet sounded, John heard a voice from the golden altar in heaven. Instructions were given to loose four angels bound at the Euphrates River. With these four angels was an army of 200 million demons mounted on horses. As they came from the abyss, the horses like demons were strange and abnormal. This demonic cavalry made use of smoke, fire and brimstone to destroy humans. This whole scene is supernatural and unnatural. Strange that this murderous campaign of judgment on unbelievers did nothing to soften their hard hearts so that they might see Christ. They refuse to repent of their devilish idolatry, nor their murder, nor their fornication and thievery.

A.W. Tozer in his book on Revelation entitled "Jesus is Victor" has this to say about the events in this terrible chapter:

> "John has been able to give us some indication of conditions and events that will take place on the earth as the final hour of settlement begins. He made it clear that the visitation of judgment upon the earth will include an invasion of supernatural powers. These will be fearsome creatures loose from the earth, and great segments of the population not only suffer but will be slain in the process.

> "I do believe the supernatural is a part of God's being an external existence. I am convinced when the living Lord of creation, the Almighty God, begins to bring this rebel world back into divine orbit, there will be an invasion from the world above as well as from the world below. And once the trumpets have sounded, sinful men and women will have no recourse. Neither will they have questions as to the origin of the judgments." (Reprinted from <u>Jesus is Victor</u> by A. W. Tozer, used by permission of WingSpread Publishers, a division of Zur Ltd.).

While the lid is off of hell and the demon hordes pour forth their venom out upon the world God Almighty is still in control. All the misery, suffering and terror of this chapter gave Satan no victory at all. The smoke soon clears away and a bright and shining angel from the throne room of God is standing stage center as the purposes of God continue to unfold.

CHAPTER SEVEN

The Big Angel and the Little Book

Revelation 10

Chapter Ten is another parenthetical chapter introducing facts about the termination of the last days and showing that Israel will have a place in these prophetic outcomes. John seems to be on the Island of Patmos when this vision comes. A very mighty angel comes into view and begins his descent to the earth. The angel was of such stature that He was able to place his right food on the sea and his left foot on the earth. Another interesting detail is given. He held in his hand a little book.

Those who study Revelation differ in their identification of this mighty angel. Some see him to be a created angel while others believe him to be Christ Himself. The word "angel" can mean a created angel or it can mean a messenger. A close study of the description of this angel supports the idea that this is Christ. The features of this angel are not usually given to angels. They are features that often identify deity. The cloud upon his head is a good example. In both the Old and the New Testaments clouds are associated with God. When the Lord Jesus ascended to heaven from the Mount of Olives the scripture says He was taken up and a cloud received Him out of their sight. Revelation 1:7 declares that at His second coming He comes with clouds and every eye shall see Him.

A rainbow was on his head. The Greek text says here that the rainbow was on his head. This was not just any rainbow but the rainbow that is clearly identified with God. One of the first things John noticed as he entered heaven was the throne of God and that there was a rainbow round about the throne. This is another mark of deity. The scripture says his face shown with light. When John saw the vision of the glorified Christ in chapter one he described his countenance as when the sun shineth in his strength (Revelation 1:16). There is similarity as to the feet of the mighty angel and Christ as observed in chapter one of Revelation.

All the above are characteristics attributed to deity and not to created angels. The speech and action of this mighty angel also bear witness that the glorified Christ is before us in this vision. His appearance at this point in the book has special significance.

The dark shadows of the demonic world followed by the decline in every aspect of circumstances on earth indicate the end is near. Christ appears and places His right foot on the sea and His left food on the earth. Someone has said those feet were nail-scarred by the cross. By this action, He announces His Second Coming and His rightful rule over the earth. How glorious will be His kingdom.

Christ the Mighty Angel then speaks with an upraised hand that "There shall be time no more." By this He meant that there will be no more delay in the fulfillment of prophecy. The mystery of God revealed to His servants, that prophecy is coming to total fulfillment.

John Eats the Little Book

The voice from heaven then instructed John to go to the Angel and take the little book from his hand. The angel told him to eat the book and advised him it would be sweet to his taste but bitter to his stomach. After John had eaten the book the angel said to him, "Thou must prophesy again before many peoples and nations, and tongues and Kings." The Greek text says John would prophesy "about" these people and nations rather than "before" them. This gives some indication of why John had to eat the "little book." A very literal translation of the "little book" would be the "little Scripture." It will contain scriptures from the Old Testament prophets that relate to the future of Israel. It should be noticed as John ate the little book, it was sweet to his taste. When he had swallowed the book it became bitter. Prophecy is both sweet and bitter. The sweet part of these prophecies is clear promises for full restoration. The bitter describes the suffering Israel will yet know during the tribulation. A.C. Gabelein says of the "Little Book,"

> "It is not a sealed book, but open. It stand for the prophecies of the Old Testament relating specifically to Israel during the time of the great tribulation, what is yet to come upon the earth, culminating in the personal and glorious appearing of the Lord to begin His millennial reign. But we do not need to say more. We saw the contents of the seven sealed books in chapter five were made known when the Lamb opened the seals. The contents of the

little book we shall also know. What follows after the parenthesis takes us upon Jewish ground and shows the fulfillment of these prophecies" (A.C. Gabelein, The Revelation, Our Hope, 1915, page 67).

John's Future Prophecies

The Angel's words to John at the close of chapter ten begin to make sense. John will certainly prophesy about many end-time situations before the great Patmos visions are finished. Israel's place in the last days will be made very clear. God will not fail to keep the unconditional promises made to the patriarch Abraham. The Son of David will sit on the throne in Jerusalem and Israel will have her place in the millennial kingdom.

This chapter gives a background for the visions of chapters 11 and 12 showing Israel's place in the final days of the tribulation and God's special provisions for them.

CHAPTER
EIGHT

Israel's Place in the End Time

Revelation 11 and 12

In the next vision the apostle John was given a reed and told by an Angel to measure the Temple of God and in particular the alter area with them that worship therein. He was further advised not to measure the court without the Temple which was given to the Gentiles. The Angel revealed to John at this time that the Gentiles would tread underfoot Jerusalem for forty-two months (3 ½ years). This vision will take place at the middle of the tribulation.

This passage confirms the Jews will be resident in Jerusalem at this time and will have reconstructed their Temple and restored

Temple worship. The Angel's message to John indicates a difficult time is about to confront the Jews when antichrist's control will intensify for the last half of the tribulation period. The measuring performed by John draws attention to the political situation. The times of the Gentiles are not over and Israel is about to feel the force of that reality.

The Current Jewish Situation

In modern times, Zionism and other factors have brought a significant Jewish population to the land of Israel and the holy city. In May of 1948 Israel became an independent country. The small nation has had the attention of the world since its birth. The very existence of the nation of Israel proves the prediction of the prophets to be true. Israel in the last days is returning to the land in a state of unbelief. Her presence in the Middle East is constant irritation to the Islamic nations. These Islamic nations do not hesitate to state their desire to annihilate the nation of Israel. The little nation of Israel is a "hot potato" for the United Nations, the European Union, Washington, DC and other Western powers.

God alone has an answer for the tension in the Middle East. He is not through with Israel nor shall He ever be. Right on planet Earth and in time and space and history God will work out His will for Israel. How God will bring this about is certainly a part of the message of the book of Revelation.

The Last Jewish Prophets

Related to the announcement of the Gentile domination of Jerusalem was the announcement of God's two witnesses whose ministry will be for 1,260 days in the holy city. William R. Newell called the two witnesses the last of the prophets. Their work will be to pour out judgment and to prophesy. God calls them His witnesses. They will boldly bear testimony during the dreadful days of tribulation to the righteousness and justice of God as well as the gospel of Jesus Christ and His kingdom which is about to come.

Many efforts have been made to identify these two witnesses as Old Testament prophets, usually Moses and Elijah. The Scripture does not name the witnesses but it does give a key to their identification. Revelation 11:4 says, "These are the two olive trees and the two candelabras standing before the God of the earth." The coming of the two witnesses was prophesied in the book of Zechariah 4:2-6. The appearance and ministry of thee two Jewish witnesses was not an innovation but planned by God and will be carried out by God during the great tribulation.

The ministry of the two witnesses will be attended by extraordinary power, the power of the Spirit of God. The power of God will be displayed in their prophecy. Mighty supernatural manifestations will characterize the work of the two witnesses as they deal with their enemies. They will stop rain, turn water to blood, and bring devastating plagues on the earth. While the two witnesses are to be in Jerusalem the effects of their ministry will be experienced through the world. An intense hatred will build up against these godly prophets.

During the 1,260 days allotted to their work they are safe and secure regardless of the enmity all around them. Like the 144,000 Jewish evangelists with the seal of God on their foreheads, they were invulnerable through their ministry. Verse seven says, that when the two witnesses finish their work the Antichrist will make war on them resulting in their death.

The public reaction to their death shows the low level of morality prevailing among the earth-dwellers with the exception of the tribulation Saints. The bodies of these godly men will be left lying in the street while a worldwide celebration takes place.

People will enjoy looking at their dead bodies, probably by television. Gifts will be exchanged to rejoice in the death of the prophets. A hilarious insanity will promote this pseudo-celebration for 3 ½ days. At that time the Bible says the Spirit of life from God enters those battered corpses lying unburied in the street. They are immediately resurrected from the dead and then raptured to heaven before the startled eyes of the watching world. John describes it thus, "And they heard a great voice from heaven saying unto them, come up hither. And they ascended up to heaven in a cloud; and their enemies beheld them" (Revelation, 11:12).

The Great Earthquake

The same hour of the rapture of the two witnesses an incredible earthquake strikes Jerusalem. The intensity of this disaster was so great that one-tenth of the city was destroyed and 7,000 men were killed. So severe was the destruction that even the wicked gave glory to God. They did not repent or yield to God but for this time only they were so struck with fear they admitted God's glory. The earthquake was the second woe announced previously by an Angel. The third woe was yet to come.

At this point the parenthetical passage ends and the sequence of trumpet judgments is resumed. The seventh angel sounded his trumpet and a voice speaks from heaven with the following announcement, "The kingdoms of this world are become the kingdoms of the Lord, and His Christ and He shall reign forever and ever." Immediately the twenty-four elders in the throne room of heaven left their thrones and fell on their faces before God worshipping and thanking Him for taking His great power and beginning to reign.

Revelation 11:15, 19 give a very brief digest of the events that will bring in Christ's millennial kingdom. Christ will descend from heaven and confront the angry nations of the world in the battle of Armageddon. There will be resurrection, judgments and rewards that follow. Revelation 19:11-21 pictures these events as they will occur at Christ's coming.

The last verse of chapter eleven deserves careful attention for it demonstrates God's concern for His people Israel at this desperate hour. The Temple of God is opened in heaven displaying the Ark of the Covenant. Many unusual physical manifestations follow this action. The Great Tribulation is now in full force. In these most dreadful days of the tribulation God remembered His covenant with Israel. The glory of her restoration is now imminent. Christ, the greater son of David, is about to take his throne. It is then the Holy Spirit will be poured out on regathered Israel and the nation will be saved in a day.

Paul wrote of this very situation in Romans 11:25, 26:

> "For I would not, brethren, that ye should be ignorant of this mystery, lest ye should be wise in your own conceits; that blindness in part is happened to Israel, until the fullness of the Gentiles be come in. And so all Israel shall be saved: as it is written, there shall come out of Sion the Deliverer, and shall turn away ungodliness from Jacob."

Note this Scripture underscores the fact made known in Revelation that Israel's full restoration will take place at the end of the times of the Gentiles, at the Second Coming of Christ.

The Vision of the Woman with the Sun

> "And there appeared a great wonder in heaven a woman clothed with the sun, and the moon under her feet, and upon her head a crown of twelve stars: And there appeared another wonder in heaven; and behold a great red dragon, having seven heads and ten horns, and seven crowns upon his heads. And his tail drew the third part of the stars of heaven, and did cast them to the earth: and the dragon stood before the woman which was ready to be delivered, for to devour her child as soon as it was born. And she brought forth a man child, who was to rule

all nations with a rod of iron: and her child was caught up unto God, and *to* his throne. And the woman fled into the wilderness, where she hath a place prepared of God, that they should feed her there a thousand two hundred *and* threescore days" (Revelation 12:1-6).

The symbolic language used to picture the woman in this vision and her situation indicates that she represents the nation of Israel. She is clothed with the sun, and the moon is under her feet and on her head wears a crown of twelve stars. An incident in the life of Joseph recorded in Genesis 37:9 offers the key to this symbol. Joseph had a dream that predicted Israel in the latter days. The sun, moon and stars bow to Joseph. His brothers were very angry at Joseph but as the Word declares they all lived to see the day when they bowed to Joseph. The sun, moon and stars do no represent the church but the covenant nation of Israel. The woman in this vision is Israel. It is without question that Israel gave us Christ through the tribe of Judah in the lineage of David.

The "man child" in the vision is clearly identified as Christ for He is destined to rule the nations with a rod of iron. The creature called the Dragon waits to devour the "man child." The term "Dragon" is used twelve times in the book of Revelation and is one of the names of Satan. The appearance of Satan in this scene pictures the darkest and cruelest side of the enemy. It is amazing that the Dragon is red in color depicting his fiendish love of death and blood. He has ten heads and seven crowns upon his head. The "man child" is rescued by divine intervention and is caught up to heaven.

The Scripture says the Dragon's tail drew one-third of the stars of heaven and cast them to the earth. Stars have already been used to designate Angels in Revelation. This indicates that Satan, a very high-ranking Angel himself, when he fell, attracted as many as one-third of the Angels in heaven. This huge number of angels turned to demons, made up the Satanic forces of evil in the world today.

The Dragon was defeated in his effort to devour the "man child." So he redirects his efforts at the woman. She immediately flew to the wilderness where God makes provision for her safety. The woman was kept there for 1,260 days (three and a half years).

The woman in the wilderness depicts the experience of the Jews during the last half of the tribulation. The Word says that God has a place for the woman's safe-keeping and also will care for her nourishment while there. Many expositors of this passage believe the site for protecting the Jews during those days will be the ancient city of Petra.

War in Heaven

The war in heaven between the Angels of the Lord under Michael and the fallen Angels led by the Dragon will take place at the beginning of the last half of the tribulation. Michael, Daniel tells us, was the Archangel assigned to the interests of Israel. This war had to do with the welfare of Israel and the coming of the millennial kingdom. Satan and his Angels lost the battle and were cast down to the earth.

Another victory won over Satan in this war and celebrated by the heavenly host was the removal of Satan from his position as accuser of the brethren. In the past he had carried on this activity day and night with this victory over the satanic forces it could be said, "Now is come salvation, and strength, and the kingdom of God, and the power of his Christ…" (Revelation 12:10). The war just fought had closed the door to the accuser of the brethren. He no longer could come before God to accuse the Saints. John includes this point in the wonderful formula by which Satan had been defeated across the centuries by the Saints.

> "And they overcome sainted by the blood of the lamb, and by the word of their testimony; and they loved not their lives unto death" (Revelation 12:11).

The awful woe to the inhabitants of the earth has now arrived. Angered by his defeat Satan vents his wrath on the earth-dwellers with a vengeance because he knows his time is short. Satan without hesitation begins to persecute the remnant of Jews still remaining in Jerusalem and other parts of the land of Israel. These had not fled earlier as described in verse six. God makes supernatural means of escape to the wilderness for this remnant. Satan counter-attacks with a flood but the earth swallowed the flood to help the woman (Jewish remnant).

Angered by his defeat, Satan returned to make war with "the remnant of her seed." It is said of this group that they keep the Commandments of God and have the testimony of Jesus Christ. Who then is the remnant of her seed? It is obvious that they are Jewish believers in Christ. They are faithful to the Gospel; await the coming of Christ and the establishment of His Kingdom. Satan will lose the battle with this remnant as well. Armageddon is just around the corner and will be his final downfall.

CHAPTER
NINE

The Beast and the False Prophet

Revelation 13

John was standing on the seashore when in a vision he sees a beast rise out of the sea. The literal translation of the Greek word here translated "beast," is a wild beast. A detailed description given of the beast indicates it represents a human being of extraordinary power and wickedness.

Some of the details show him to be the ruler of the revived Roman Empire. The ten crowns indicate a ten-nation Confederacy that will give the beast political power in fulfillment of the prophecy given in Daniel Chapter 2. Nebuchadnezzar saw in a dream a great image that he learned through Daniel depicted the whole times of the Gentiles from Babylon until Christ's second coming. The ten toes of that image revealed the concept of a ten-nation Confederacy in the area of the ancient Roman Empire in the last day. It will be destroyed by the kingdom of God that will begin rule at Christ's second coming (Daniel 2:24, 45).

The beast is otherwise known as the antichrist. The purpose of this chapter is to reveal the background of this wicked dictator of the revived Roman Empire. Verse two shows characteristics of the rulers of the major gentile empires of the ancient world. The same animals are used to describe the nature of this beast, the leopard, the bear and the lion.

This verse also gives the source of the beast's power, his political position and authority. All of it comes directly from Satan, here again called the Dragon. In verse five, Satan gives the beast authority to continue for another 3 ½ years (Revelation 6:2). During the seven years of the great tribulation the world will be ruled by a demon possessed moral maniac.

The antichrist's public image will be built up by an act of pseudo-supernaturalism. One of his heads was wounded to death and the deadly wound was healed. Verse two indicates the supposed miracle caused the whole world population to be amazed. That amazement soon turns to worship of Satan for they attributed the supposed healing to him. This built up the confidence of the people in the beast's political and military powers.

In 3 ½ years we have moved from deception and diplomacy to an all-out totalitarian government. Satan equips him with powers of persuasion and oratory that mesmerizes the populace. His pronouncements were filled with blasphemy. He reneges on his treaty with Israel and desecrates the Temple, setting himself up as God. This brought an end to the Jewish worship in the Temple and opened the Jews to persecution. It is to this awful event that Jesus speaks in the Olivet discourse.

"When ye therefore shall see the abomination of desolation, spoken of by Daniel the prophet, stand in the holy place, (whoso readeth, let him understand:) Then let them which be in Judaea flee into the mountains" (Matthew 24:15-16).

How helpful these words will be to the suffering Jewish remnant. Many will flee the Jerusalem area heading for the wilderness where God will care for them. The antichrist will show his real intention as this awful "abomination of desolation" takes place. Instead of being Israel's friend he will be their worst enemy.

Antichrist will not only blaspheme God's name and His Temple and everything heavenly he will make war on the saints and overcome them. By this time antichrist will have total international rule with millions of deceived souls who will actually worship him.

The Saints are clearly defined here as "all whose names are found written in the book of life of the Lamb slain from the foundation of the world." To these saints verse nine is directed as a warning to abide faithful no matter the cost.

The tenth verse is an undeniable instruction to the Saints to be nonresistance during the tribulation. They are urged to rather than resist accept what comes with perseverance and faith. There is much for contemporary believers to learn from the tribulation Saints.

The False Prophet

The beast (antichrist) came out of the sea which symbolizes the people. Another beast appears from the earth (which can also be translated as the land meaning Israel). The second beast is probably Jewish. The second beast has two horns like a lamb but he speaks like a dragon. He exercises the power of the beast from out of the sea. The second beast devotes his attention to the interest of the first beast. Some consider the second beast to be the antichrist but the passage gives him a secondary role. His passion is the promotion of the beast from the sea who is the Antichrist.

He bears the name false prophet for he deceives the earth-dwellers by his pseudo-miracles and artistry at witchcraft. He makes an image of the beast and appears to give it life, and enables it to speak. The next step in his plan is teaching the deceived earth-dwellers to worship the beast.

The false prophet devises a plan of total control of all people. In order to do business, to buy and to sell one must have the Mark of the beast, the number of his name.

The outward appearance of the false prophet suggests that he has an interest in religion. The antichrist system was not void of religion. For most of the reign of Antichrist his kingdom has a diabolical religion that can only be called blasphemy. The worship of Antichrist was at the heart of this wicked system. This accounts for the horns of a lamb on the false prophet. The incarnation, deity, death, resurrection and ascension of Christ will be imitated by the lies and pseudo-miracles of the counterfeit prophet. The worship of the antichrist is at the heart of this evil religion.

The full makeup of this religion is discussed in Revelation chapter 17. The false prophet will blend the ideas of the apostate churches both Catholic and Protestant. This counterfeit church is presented as a Scarlet woman the epitome of wickedness. She is sitting on the beast. The false prophet will be the genius behind this darkness.

The time will come when the religious system will be destroyed by Antichrist and the false prophet. The account of this action will be considered in the 17th chapter of Revelation.

The final verse of chapter 13 deals with the number of the beast. Many scholarly efforts have gone into solving the mystery of the number 666. They are mostly without success. The answer to this question will become evident to those who are alive upon earth while the beast is ruling? The answer does not lie in history but in the future day of the great tribulation. The meaning will become evident to the tribulation Saints. The number will identify the beast so those who are committed to Christ will not be deceived by him or his wicked system. They will choose martyrdom rather than submit to antichrist.

John Bright calls this group the "enlightened remnant." Enabled by the Holy Spirit they will detect the lie and stay true to Jesus whatever the cost.

The parenthetical information in this chapter regards the antichrist, the false prophet and the revived Roman Empire. It is at this mid-tribulation point the real character and purpose of the antichrist are made clear.

CHAPTER
TEN

Forecasts of Victory

Revelation 14, 15

The visions of chapter nine and thirteen are the darkest and most dreadful in the book of Revelation. What a spiritual uplift it must've been for the apostle John when his eyes saw the Lamb of God standing with the 144,000 who had the Father's name written on their foreheads. This company is standing on Mount Zion. They are the same 144,000 that were sealed as the servants of God in chapter seven. Those Jewish evangelists made it through tribulation because of God's protection over them and now stand in the presence of Christ.

On which mount Zion does the scene take place? Is it the one in Jerusalem or is there a mount Zion in heaven? This is the only mention of mount Zion in the book of Revelation. The Lamb is standing on Mount Zion in Jerusalem with this Jewish throng who have been his footstep followers during the great tribulation. This company is not the church but the faithful Jewish servants who have triumphantly made it through the tribulation period. This vision is a forecast of Christ's great victory coming soon on the Earth. It predicts what will occur at the time of Christ's second coming which is about to happen.

John heard a voice form heaven as the scene on mount Zion came into view. Thunder crashed with the sound of many waters. The sound of harpers harping was also heard. A new song was then heard before the throne. No one could learn it except the 144,000.

Dean Alford helps in comprehending this vision when he points out the singing had its origins with harpers in heaven. Alford says, "I would call the attention of the reader to the fact, essential to the right understanding of the vision, that the harpers and the song are in heaven, and the 144,000 on Earth." He further contends that only the 144,000 join the song for they had fully followed the Lamb and knew personally the trials, joy, and purity of heart the servants of God experience (Dean Alford, Greek New Testament, volume IV, Cambridge, Deighten, Bell and Co. 1871, page 695).

The next two verses give a picture of the true godliness of this group of Jewish Saints. They are called the "firstfruits unto God and to the Lamb." By this is meant that an innumerable host of Jews and gentiles would yet be saved during the remainder of the tribulation. The harvest is not over. Many of these will make up the population of the earth at the start of the millennium. Dr. Ironside calls these firstfruits, the firstfruits of the kingdom.

The Angel with the Everlasting Gospel

The second vision in this chapter was of an angel flying in the midst of heaven preaching the everlasting gospel to the earth-dwellers. Angels have never preached the gospel before. It has been throughout the church age the responsibility of believers to preach the gospel. The Angel is not preaching another gospel for the word of God forbids that. He is preaching selects aspects of the gospel to the truth resisting people on earth. The message the Angel preaches will be to the entire world.

With a voice that can be heard everywhere as he admonishes them to fear God and give glory to Him for the awful hour of judgment is imminent. The people are urged to recognize God as the creator and therefore worship Him. The Angels message touches the gospel issues that relate to heart conditions of the spiritual rebellion in Christ haters.

Babylon has Fallen

Third vision comes as another forecast of the soon coming victory of Christ and his kingdom. An angel announces that the great city of Babylon that corrupts the whole world is fallen. The complete details of this judgment will be considered in chapter 18.

Doom for Those Who Worship the Beast

A third Angel makes his appearance with a loud voice advising those unbelieving multitudes on earth of the doom about to come on them because they have worshipped the Antichrist and received his mark. It is implied by this angelic announcement that time has run out for the Antichrist and God Almighty is about to intervene.

The description of the doom awaiting those rebels is frightening. God has prepared the wine of his wrath and each of them must drink of it. The result of their rejection of the grace of God will be torment with fire and brimstone before holy Angels and the Lamb for ever and ever. For all the countless ages of eternity they have no possibility of ever knowing rest again.

This hopeless picture is immediately followed by the testimony of the tribulation Saints. In contrast to the doomed earth-dwellers the tribulation Saints are known for their endurance, obedience, and vital faith in the power of Jesus. They continue in confidence doing the Commandments of the Lord Jesus Christ.

The Blessed State of the Holy Dead

John was instructed from heaven to write, "Blessed are the dead which die in the Lord from henceforth: yea, saith the spirit, that they may rest from their labors; and their works do follow them" (Revelation 14:13).

Here is another forecast of the coming defeat of Antichrist and the immediate victory of Jesus Christ. In this situation the unbelieving have no hope but the believing tribulation Saints have blessed hope. The martyrs die joyfully for glory is just ahead of them.

A Forecast of Armageddon

The final battle and victory which brings to a close the great tribulation is the battle of Armageddon. Verses 14 to 20 of chapter 14 give a prophetic forecast for the outcome of Armageddon. It is pictured as a harvest. One like the Son of Man with a gold crown and a sharp sickle was told to bring in the harvest of the earth for it is right for harvest. The Angel uses the sickle to reap the earth. Jesus' teaching in Matthew 13:41 will be fulfilled when the Angel carries out the harvest judgment.

The second Angel comes out of the Temple in heaven also having a sharp sickle. Yet another Angel comes out of the altar in the temple located in heaven who tells the Angel with a sharp sickle to gather in the vintage of the Earth. He gathers the vine and cast it into the winepress of the wrath of God. The winepress was stomped outside the city, meaning Jerusalem. The bloodshed at this battle will be as deep as horses' bridles and will flow over an area of some 200 miles. The visions of the harvest forecast the battle of Armageddon which takes place after Christ and the armies of heaven come out of the glory and descend to the Earth. The details of this final battle will be found in the nineteenth chapter of Revelation.

At the close of this battle the great tribulation will be over. Christ will actually be on earth and bringing order out of universal chaos. Chapter fourteen is full of hope and comfort for the tribulation Saints. The tribulation judgments are almost finished. The seven bowls of wrath remain and will be carried out in a short period of time. The victory of the Lamb can be seen on the horizon.

Chapter fifteen fills in some remaining details as to what must take place before Armageddon. Here remains one more series of seven judgments to be poured out on the Earth before Christ returns. John saw an extraordinary sign in heaven intended to open even more the apostles' understanding of how the wrath of God will work in the end time. Seven Angels appear to execute the seven vials of wrath. These plagues will complete the full twenty-one judgments that take place during the seven years of the great tribulation.

John became aware of more activity in heaven. He saw a sea of glass mingled with fire. Standing on the sea were all who had triumphed over the beast. They had harps of God and were singing the song of Moses and the song of the lamb. They were worshiping the Lord God Almighty whom they address as King of saints.

The words of their heavenly hymn indicate the Saints were very much aware of the imminent thousand year reign of Christ.

As the scene changes John witnesses the opening of the tabernacle of the testimony in heaven. Seven Angels came out of the Temple. Their clothing was pure white linen and golden girdles. The details of their dress dictate that they are acting out of the righteousness of God. The bowls of wrath they pour out on Earth will be acts of the justice of God.

One of the four living creatures before the throne of God gave to the Angels seven golden bowls of the wrath of God. The Temple was soon filled with smoke from the glory of God. No man could enter the Temple until the Angels had completed the delivery of the seven bowls of wrath. It is noteworthy that the bowls were of gold symbolizing the deity and the glory of God. The smoke in the Temple is the Shekinah glory of God that came on the tabernacle in the Old Testament.

It is of more than passing interest that in this short chapter prior to the releasing of the bowls of wrath such attention is given to the names and works of God. His works are called great and marvelous; his ways are true; his character is holy. How fitting the song of the Lamb against this picture of the impending wrath. The song of the tribulation Saints sounds through the heavens as they worship the Lord God Almighty.

The seven Angels go forth to their works with songs of victory through Christ ringing in their ears.

CHAPTER
ELEVEN

Count Down to Armageddon

Revelation 16

A great voice from the Temple called for the seven angels to pour the bowls of the wrath of God on the earth. As each angel does his work the devastation of the Earth becomes greater.

The First Bowl of Wrath

The nature of the first bowl was very painful as distressing sores broke out on the bodies of the apostates on earth. It was a judgment of their rejection of Jesus Christ and their acceptance of the Antichrist.

The Second Bowl of Wrath

The sea becomes the target of the second bowl of God's wrath. The sea was made like the blood of a dead man and every living thing in it dies.

The Third Bowl of Wrath

The third bowl of God's wrath is directed at all the fresh water on Earth corrupting it with blood. The magnitude of this disaster is hard to imagine. When this judgment takes place "the Angels of the waters" declare the justice of God in taking this action. "The angels of the waters" are evidently Angels assigned to this aspect of the natural world. The justice of God's action was vengeance for the murder of the saints and prophets. These Angels conclude that the apostate earth-dwellers are altogether worthy of such divine action. There also came a voice out of the altar in heaven declaring the acts of God in this bowl of wrath to be true and righteous.

The Fourth Bowl of Wrath

The fourth angel poured out his bowl on the sun. It gave forth such power that the earth-dwellers were scorched by the excessive heat. They responded to this catastrophe by blaspheming God. The apostates would neither repent of their sin nor give God glory. They know the judgments are coming from Almighty God but that truth did not alter their intention to rebel against Him.

The Fifth Bowl of Wrath

The target of the fifth bowl of wrath is "the seat of the beast." Up until now the Antichrist has escaped the troubling judgments but the fifth bowl penetrated the very heart of his palace and headquarters. The experience will be like that of Pharaoh in the Old Testament. The Scripture says his kingdom will be covered with darkness so dreadful men will gnaw their tongues in pain. Evidently this judgment will include painful sores on their bodies. They did what only the wicked will do in such circumstances; they blaspheme God and refuse to repent. By the time of the fifth bowl of wrath the whole world has become a nightmare. The wicked burn with hatred and begin to plot the battle of Armageddon with all intensity.

The Sixth Bowl of Wrath

The results of the sixth bowl of wrath give strong evidence of a worldwide movement toward Armageddon. The bowl was poured on the river Euphrates and that body of water dries up. This will make it possible for the military forces of the Far East to move into the Middle East where Armageddon will take place.

The drying up of this mighty river symbolizes the removal of hindrances to such a military movement from the Orient.

Not only is the Euphrates dried up with the sixth bowl of the wrath of God but a movement of evil will begin to speed up preparation for the battle of Armageddon. Three unclean spirits will come out of the mouth of the dragon (Satan), out of the mouth of the beast, and out of the mouth of the false prophet. The entire evil trinity, the devil, the Antichrist and the false prophet will release demon forces that will begin to agitate the wicked toward an all out war against God. Their activity will cover all the nations of the world. All will be called to engage in the battle of the great day of God Almighty.

Demons have always had their place of activity in war. During World War I an American missionary couple was ministering in the Kansu-Tibetan border, a very remote area in that part of China. They were dealing one day with the case of demon possession. The demon spoke saying, "But we are weak because so many demons have gone to the war." This puzzled the missionaries for they had heard of no war. Only a few days after this incident they received mail from home and heard that World War I was underway.

There can be little doubt that demons are engaged in war all over our world. This condition according to Scripture will have reached its peak at the outpouring of the sixth bowl of the wrath of God.

The psalmist in Psalms describes the insanity that will attend this war fever in the last days.

> "Why do the heathen rage, and the people imagine a vain thing? The kings of the earth set themselves, and the rulers take counsel together, against the LORD, and against his anointed, *saying,* Let us break their bands asunder, and cast away their cords from us. He that sitteth in the heavens shall laugh: the Lord shall have them in derision" (Psalms 2:1-4).

Zechariah says,

> "Behold the day of the LORD cometh, and thy spoil shall be divided in the midst of thee. For I will gather all nations against Jerusalem to battle; and the city shall be taken, and the houses rifled, and the women ravished; and half of the city shall go forth into captivity, and the residue of the people shall not be cut off from the city. Then shall the LORD go forth, and fight against those nations, as when he fought in the day of the battle" (Zechariah 14:1-3).

Zechariah tells us that though the demons are stirring up this war spirit against God, the Almighty himself is really in charge and will gather the nations for this battle.

In Revelation 16:15, Christ interrupts the narrative to remind the readers that He is coming suddenly and unexpectedly. He then gives John a beatitude that relates to His second coming.

"Blessed is he that watcheth and keepeth his garments, lest he walk naked, and they see his shame." What a challenge to be among the watchers in these last days. Prophecy is not speculation. It is absolute truth. It is truth that should have a large place in our lives as end time believers. To live with the expectation of being an eyewitness to the victory of the Lord Jesus Christ calls for total obedience to his Lordship.

This brief word from Christ is followed up with the fact that He will gather that nations to Armageddon. All the way through Revelation, Christ is either in the center of things or working out His sovereign will on the sidelines.

The Seventh Bowl of Wrath

The hour has come for the seventh bowl of the wrath of God to be poured out. It was poured into the air and at that moment the great voice from the temple in heaven says, "It is done." These words come directly from the judgment throne. For the last time the temple in heaven is seen by John. The events that are soon to follow will bring an end to the time of the Gentiles.

A great earthquake takes place amid voices of thundering and lightning. It is greater and more damaging than any previous earthquake in the history of the world. The epicenter of this quake is the great city of Rome (Babylon). The destruction of Babylon had already been announced in Revelation 14:8.

The effect of the earthquake is universal. The cities of the Gentile nations all fall, islands and mountains are severely damaged. In addition to this earthquake, heavens rain down large hailstones that weigh as much as 100 pounds each. The Earth by this time is one huge disaster area. The ungodly apostate earth-dwellers once again resort to blaspheming God.

Before leaving this passage time must be given to the identification of Babylon. The ancient city of Babylon had its origin in the post-flood era of Bible history. It came about as a rebellion against God and a human effort to secure themselves and make their own way to heaven by the construction of the infamous Tower of Babel. Babel means confusion. Babylonian religion and politics have been the ultimate manifestation of confusion in world history.

In the days of Judah's apostasy Babylon was a powerful city, capital of a great empire. Many Jews were taken into captivity to Babylon. The empire eventually collapsed but the city continued until brought under the judgment of God. The prophet speaks of the destruction of Babylon as a direct act of God because their treatment of His people.

Isaiah prophesied,

"And Babylon, the glory of kingdoms, the beauty of the Chaldees' excellency, shall be as when God overthrew Sodom and Gomorrah. It shall never be inhabited, neither shall it be dwelt in from generation to generation: neither shall the Arabian pitch tent there, neither shall the shepherds make their fold there. But wild beasts of the desert shall lie there; and their houses shall be full of doleful creatures; and owls shall dwell there, and satyrs shall dance there. And wild beasts of the islands shall cry in their desolate houses, and dragons in *their* pleasant palaces: and her time *is* near to come, and her days shall not be prolonged" (Isaiah 13:19-22).

William Kelly says of this passage, "The past ruin of Babylon is a type of the future destruction of Rome. Thus the fall of this first great power of the Gentiles is a type of doom of the last, when Israel will have been finally set free, a converted people, being delivered spiritually as much as nationally, and thence forward made to express the glory of Jehovah upon the earth" (William Kelly, An Exposition of the book of Isaiah, Klock and Klock, fourth edition, pages 162-163).

The study of chapter 17 and 18 will help clarify that Babylon symbolizes the revived Roman Empire, the kingdoms of the Antichrist. Babylon is the name given to the hellish religious and political system of the Antichrist but its geographical capital will be the city of Rome.

The results of the earthquake brought on by the seventh bowl of the wrath are given some detail in Revelation 16:19. The first happening is the division of the great city into three parts followed by the fall of the cities of the Gentile world. Babylon the Great is next to be affected by the earthquake. It is generally assumed that the great city in the first part of the sentence and Babylon the great in the third part are one and the same city. In Revelation 11:8, Jerusalem is called "the great city" and at the rapture of the two witnesses experience an earthquake of significance but was not destroyed.

The prophet Zechariah prophesied an earthquake in Jerusalem when Christ returns and His feet stands on the Mount of Olives. The result of that earthquake will split the Mount of Olives resulting in the formation of a long valley (Zechariah 14:4).

It is evident from Revelation 16:19 that the damage in Jerusalem will be much less than the damage on Rome (Babylon) the Antichrist headquarters and the cities of the Gentiles which will be left in ruins.

CHAPTER
TWELVE

The Fall of Babylon

Revelation 17 and 18

The outpouring of the bowls of the wrath of God essentially bring the great tribulation to its close. Chapter 17 and 18 supply a full account of the ruin of Babylon. Some suppose that the ancient city of Babylon in Mesopotamia will be rebuilt and made the capital of Antichrist's government during the great tribulation. There does not seem to be support for that position in the book of Revelation. Babylon, in these two chapters, speak of the city of Rome, the headquarters of the Antichrist's government which will be in reality a revival of the old Roman empire with a ten nation confederacy that backs the reign of the Antichrist.

The language of the two chapters before us helps to clarify this interpretation. More than a government is involved in the term Babylon. It might better be defined as a religious and political system.

The heavenly angel showing John the vision of the Scarlet woman was one of the seven angels who dispensed the bowls of wrath. The angel told John he would show him the judgment of the great whore. He was then transported in the spirit into the wilderness.

In the wilderness, John saw a woman seated on a Scarlet colored beast. The beast was full of names of blasphemy and had seven heads and ten horns. This description corresponds to that given of the beast in chapter thirteen. The only additional information on the beast in the scene is the color scarlet. The beast in spite of himself has a preoccupation with religion or more accurately false religion. Like his master, the devil, he wants to be worshiped as God. It is his nature to blaspheme the true God.

Attention is given to the Scarlet woman on the back of the beast. This vision makes it evident that Antichrist will be heavily engaged in religion. The Scarlet woman is none other than the apostate church. The woman is decked with gold, valuable jewels, and pearls. She holds in her hand a golden cup full of the abomination and filthiness of her fornication.

Her name is Mystery, Babylon the Great, Mother of Harlots and Abominations of the earth. She is drunk with the blood of the saints and martyrs of Jesus. The apostle was overwhelmed by the sight of the Scarlet woman on the scarlet beast. The angel notes John's response and began immediately to explain the mystery of the woman and the beast.

Before considering what the angel says about the beast some attention should be given to the meaning of the Scarlet woman and how she fits into Bible prophecy. She is the religious system that has been in formation since Old Testament times. From the days of Cain, the idolatry, false religion and apostasy across the ages has developed the Scarlet woman. In both Testaments the Scriptures have called idolatry and any false religion spiritual adultery.

Paul wrote in his first letter to Timothy,

> "Now the Spirit speaking expressly, that in the latter times some shall depart from the faith, giving heed to seducing spirits, and doctrines of Devils, speaking lies in hypocrisy; having their conscience seared with a hot iron; for bidding to marry, and commanding to abstain from meats, which God had created to be received with Thanksgiving of them which know and believe the truth" (I Timothy 4:1-3).

Apostate religion has been in formation across most of history but in these latter times, it has accelerated. When Antichrist comes on the scene the components of the Scarlet woman will be in place. There will be Apostate Roman Catholicism, apostate Protestantism, the multiple cults that have hived off of the Christian church. It will not be difficult for apostate churches to join forces with animism, Eastern mystical religions and cultic religions of all varieties.

After the rapture there will still be apostate Christians on the earth. They will fit easily into the plans of the beast.

There are two other facts about the Scarlet woman that should be considered. Verse nine says, "The seven heads are seven mountains on which the woman sitteth." The city of Rome is always associated with seven mountains. The city of Rome will be the location of the capital of the beast kingdom and also of his apostate religion.

The last verse of chapter 17 says, "The woman which thou sawest is that great city, which reigned over the kings of the earth." The place of the Scarlet woman in the Antichrist system is very powerful. Her designation as the great city gives credence to the idea that Roman Catholicism will be the catalyst for bringing this religious system together.

The Antichrist's interest in religion appears at the very beginning of his reign with the treaty he signs with Israel. That act will make possible the construction of the temple in Jerusalem and the renewal of Judaism after the Levitical worship and sacrifice so long denied the Jews.

The Antichrist will be supported by the ten-nation Confederacy of the revived Roman Empire.

The Antichrist and the ten kings are determined to make war with the Lamb who is Lord Jesus Christ. Here is another factor in the growing military move toward Palestine and the battle of Armageddon. This Scripture says that the Lamb will overcome them and all other military powers that come to Armageddon. Christ will be victorious because He is King of Kings and Lord of Lords. The blood washed, regenerated and raptured church will be with Him in this battle. To be enlisted in the army of heaven that follows Jesus from the glory room on high to the blood-soaked battleground of Armageddon will be those He has chosen and called to Himself and they will distinguish themselves by their faithfulness to the Lord Jesus Christ.

Chapter eighteen opens with the visitation of another powerful angel from heaven. He shouts the news that Babylon is fallen and has become the habitation for demons. The inherent evil in the Babylonian system is clearly exposed to men, angels and demons. It is significant that the angel from heaven lighted up the earth with his glory. The lie of the Antichrist is now uncovered for the world to understand that the system so many had accepted was a cage for every work of darkness.

They lamented the ruin of Babylon. Their cry was that everything that meant anything to them was now gone and it took only one hour. The earth-dwellers will be so blinded by their love for sin they will ignore the truth about Antichrist and his confused and darkened civilization that has plagued their lives and now leaves them empty and hopeless.

They continue to mourn the loss of pleasure, over-indulgence, sensuality, wealth, materialism, luxury, extravagance, and drunkenness. John summarizes their agony in verse 14: "And the fruits that thy soul lusted after are departed from thee, and all things which were dainty and goodly are departed from thee, thou shalt find them no more at all" (Revelation 18:14).

The effect of the fall of Babylon is universal. It touches the leadership of the world; tradesmen, the artisan, the merchant, those engaged in transporting goods, the ordinary laborer. The whole economic and social system of planet earth comes to a screeching halt.

Even at this late hour of the great tribulation, a faithful minority will still be resisting the system of the Antichrist. Another angel speaks a word to them saying, "Come out of her my people, that ye be not partakers of her sins, and that ye receive not of her plagues" (Revelation 18:4). This is a clear call to separation from the soul damning system with which the culture of that day will be saturated by the Antichrist and his demon associates.

The second Angel's admonition has been revealed here for not only the remnant in the last hours of the great tribulation but for every generation of Christians since the Book of Revelation became available.

Those believers that are awake to the imminent coming of Christ will be moved to seek holiness and true separation from the world as they await Christ's coming. As the apostle John wrote in his first epistle, "Everyone that had this hope in him purifies himself even as he is pure" (I John 3:3).

The call to separation is never just negative. He who separates from apostasy and worldliness is also called to a positive separation unto God. The writer of Hebrews states it so succinctly, "Let us go forth therefore unto him without the camp bearing his reproach" (Hebrews 13:13).

Walter Scott, a British Bible teacher of the early 20th century comments on Revelation 18:4, "The call is imperative. Babylon is a system that cannot be remodeled on scriptural lines, and hence there is ever but one course open to the faithful – one of thorough separation from that which falsely bears the name of Christ" (Walter Scott, <u>Exposition of the book of Revelation of Jesus Christ,</u> Fleming Revel, no date, no copyright).

This eighteenth chapter show God to be intent on the destruction of the city. It talks about how God Almighty in one stroke tears to pieces the diabolical civilization of the Antichrist.

The city here called Babylon is the city of Rome where the government of Antichrist will be situated during the great tribulation. From the revived Roman Empire and with its support, his rule will eventually cover the entire world. This is confirmed in chapter 17:9, which states the Scarlet woman in union with Antichrist are located in the seven hills of Roman.

Dean Alford, British Greek scholar says, "By these words no less plainly then verse 18, Rome is pointed out" (Dean Alford, Greek New Testament volume IV, page 709).

Another scholar who speaks to the concept of literal Babylon being rebuilt as the Antichrist's capital city is William Kelly, a leading Pre-millenarian in the 19th century. He says of the notion of rebuilding Babylon,

> "Some have though there will be a reestablishment of Oriental Babylon in the last days. They suppose there will be a literal city on the plains of Shinar. This appears to be fundamentally false. The New Testament points out by evident marks what the future will be; and in order apparently to guard against that illusion, even contrasts the apocalyptic Babylon in some respects with that of

the Chaldees. The Babylon of the Old World was built upon a plain; the future Babylon is characterized by the seven Mountains it sits on" (William Kelly, <u>Exposition on the Book of Isaiah</u>, Klock and Klock reprint, pages 164, 165).

Kelly later concludes that the past ruin of Babylon is the type of the future ruin of Rome, the seat of the Antichrist government.

A Divine View of Babylon Ruin

Heaven is called upon to rejoice at the total collapse of Babylon. Certain saints are called upon to do the rejoicing. "The holy apostles and prophets have this privilege for God has taken vengeance on the wicked system for their sakes."

As the rejoicing took place in heaven a mighty angel cast what looked like a millstone into the sea and announced, "Thus with violence shall that great city Babylon be thrown down, and shall be found no more at all." Thus shall all the voices of Babylon be silenced forever. All activity will cease. Then her lights will go out. They found in her the blood of the prophets and saints and martyrs. It was discovered that her power and influence came by sorcery. Therefore Almighty God brought her down to total ruin and closes the door on Babylon forever.

CHAPTER
THIRTEEN

Christ's Return and Reign on Earth

Revelation 19 and 20

As the millstone splashed in the sea, the curtain went down on Babylon. John's attention was immediately attracted to an outburst of praise and worship from the angels and saints in heaven. The heavenly host were fully aware of the judgment God meted out to the great city of Babylon. Their song was an affirmation of God's righteous judgment on the Scarlet woman and the Antichrist's wretched system of demonic darkness. This night is about to end and the "Sun of Righteousness arises with healing in his wings" (Malachi 4:2).

The blessed refrain in their song was, "Alleluia, for the Lord God omnipotent reigneth." Christ is about to assume his rightful throne in the presence of the whole universe. The prayer so often uttered is about to be answered, "Thy kingdom come... On Earth as it is in heaven."

The Marriage and Marriage Supper of the Lamb.

The church, the Bride of Christ, was raptured to heaven prior to the beginning of the great tribulation. Now the time has arrived for this greatest of all marriages. No details are given of this event. The reader is told that the wife made herself ready for the marriage.

The Scriptures say that it was granted her to be clothed in fine linen, clean and white. Then the Scriptures explained that this fine linen is the righteousness of the saints. In preparation for the marriage the bride appears before the judgment seat of Christ. Her life is reviewed and rewarded. All her clothing for the marriage comes by the grace of God. Surely the words of Paul in Ephesians 5:27 are fulfilled. "That He might present it to himself a glorious church, not having spot or wrinkle, or any such thing: but that it should be holy and without blemish."

The marriage is followed by the marriage supper of the Lamb. There will be guests present for the supper. They will be made up of Old Testament saints, martyrs and tribulation saints.

The love feast practiced in the apostolic church and by many churches in our day is a type of the marriage supper of the Lamb. The bread and the cup also have eschatological dimension. The apostle said, "For as often as you eat this bread, and drink this cup, ye do shew the Lord's death till he come." If we celebrate communion without reflection on the future Christ has planned for us, we have overlooked a great blessing we should enjoy every time we come to the Lord's Table. There is a sense in which the communion ought always to be a dress rehearsal for the rapture and the marriage supper of the Lamb.

Before leaving the scene of the marriage supper of the Lamb it would be profitable to reflect on the ancient prophecy of this wedding in Psalm 45. The Psalmist speaks of this prophecy as a good matter. What a magnificent picture he brings of the King and His wife. Emphasis is placed on moral and spiritual grandeur of the King and for that reason the Father has blessed them forever. What we know about Christ in this Psalm covers important aspects of the transition from the heavenly scene to His return to earth riding as a conqueror. Psalm 45:3-6 pictures Christ's incredible public entrance to the earth's atmosphere eventually in the establishment of His millennial kingdom.

What great credentials Christ has for His holy office. The Psalmist says, "Thou lovest righteousness and hated wickedness; therefore thy God, has anointed thee with the old of gladness above thy fellows."

The marriage and the marriage supper of the Lamb will take place in heaven before the return of Christ to the earth.

John is told to write the fourth beatitude in Revelation. It says, "Blessed are they which are called unto the marriage supper of the Lamb." The angel then told John what he had just written were the true sayings of God.

The aged apostle was so moved by the angel's words that he knelt at his feet to worship him. The angel stopped him and advised John that he was his fellow servant and of his brethren that have the testimony of Jesus. He told John to worship God for the testimony of Jesus is the spirit of prophecy. This interlude John experienced with the angel puts this whole series of events in divine perspective. It is significant that the angel used the name Jesus, the name given Him in His incarnation. From chapter one it was made evident that the object of this book was the unveiling of Jesus Christ. The virgin born son of God was the fulfillment of innumerable prophecies across the ages. At the close of His earthly journey of 33 ½ years He returns to heaven and awaits the close of history, the consummation of the ages. His personal return to earth and His kingdom is fulfilled in His 1,000 years reign over all the earth. All of the prophetic events center in Christ. He beyond question is the spirit of prophecy.

The Coming of the Bridegroom and His Bride

John testifies to seeing heaven opened and sees the departure of Christ, His bride and the angels coming toward earth. Christ is leading the procession mounted on a white horse. There is something of a footnote here saying of Christ that He is faithful and true. He judges and makes war in righteousness. What a contrast to the military movement on earth where the Antichrist and the deceived leaders of the Gentile world lead their forces to Armageddon.

Every detail given of Christ shows His perfections and superiority to all others. His vestment is dipped in blood no doubt splashed from the conflict in which He is riding. Among the names given Christ is the Word of God. Out of His mouth is a sharp sword. This is the Word of God by which He will succeed in the defeat of the Gentile nations and their demon-driven dictators.

John is about to see the victory which the Holy Spirit showed Enoch back in the dawn of history. Enoch prophesied, "Behold the Lord cometh with 10,000 of his saints, to execute judgment upon all." The great armies following Christ out of heaven are also mounted on white horses. They are the church saints and the angels. Christ is bringing His bride with Him. She will be with her Lord when He defeats the foe. She will be present when He takes over the kingdoms of this world. More is learned of the role of the church as the events of chapter twenty are made known.

The Battle of Armageddon

Some details are given in verse fifteen as to how Christ will engage this vast army assembled in the Valley of Megiddo north of Jerusalem. With the sword He will smite the nations. With wrath Christ will tread these enemy forces like grapes in a wine vat. The immediate effect of Christ's strategy will be the total devastation of the military power of the Gentile nations.

John saw an angel standing in the sun who called all the fowls to gather for what Scripture calls the "supper of the great God." They are summoned to eat the flesh of all who will be killed in this awful battle. There will not be a single wound or fatality in the armies from heaven that follow Christ.

The apostle Paul wrote to the church at Thessalonica about this battle. Paul said, "And to you who are troubled rest with us, when the Lord Jesus shall be revealed from heaven with His mighty angels."

"In flaming fire taking vengeance on them that know not God, and that obey not the gospel of our Lord Jesus Christ."

"Who shall be punished with everlasting destruction from the presence of the Lord, and form the glory of his power; when he shall come to be glorified in his saints, and to be admired in all them that believe (because our testimony among you was believed) in that day" (2 Thessalonians 1:9,10).

The power and glory of Christ completely overcomes in a short time the greatest military force ever assembled in the history of the world. Christ apprehends both the antichrist and the false prophet and casts them alive directly into the lake of fire. Christ slew all the Gentile kings gathered for this battle and left the bodies for the vultures to devour.

The Son of God came to the world at His incarnation as gentle as a lamb. He gave himself as the Savior of the world. Christ gave no resistance to the ungodly who tortured and crucified Him. When He returns as King of kings and Lord of lords He will subjugate the nations of the world and bring an end to the diabolical work of the trinity of evil.

Christ is fully victorious at the battle of Armageddon and will be ready to initiate the blessed rule of the kingdom of heaven on earth.

The Millennial Reign of Christ

When the reader of the Revelation comes to the 20th chapter he has arrived at the apex of the doctrine of the second coming of

Jesus Christ to the earth. It is time to raise the question, Why is Christ returning to the world? Is He coming to subjugate all evil at the battle of Armageddon? Is He returning to recall Israel to her homeland and restore her spiritually and politically? Is He coming to judge the wicked? All of these things and more will Christ do when He returns but these things are only preliminary to His major work. Christ is returning primarily to reign as King of kings over all the nations of the world for 1,000 years.

The second Psalm in the Old Testament gives the account of the coronation of the Lord Jesus Christ as King. Beginning at verse six it reads, "Yet have I set my king upon my holy hill of Zion. I will declare the decree; the Lord has said unto me, thou art my son; this day I have begotten thee. Ask of thee, and I shall give thee the heathen for thine inheritance, and the outermost part of the earth for thy possession. Thou shall break them with a rod of iron; thou shall dash them in pieces like a potter's vessel. Be wise now therefore, o ye Kings; be instructed, you judges of the earth. Serve the Lord with fear, and rejoice with trembling. Kiss the son, lest he be angry and ye perish from the way, when his wrath is kindled but a little. Blessed are all they that put their trust in Him" (Psalms 2:6-12).

Chapter twenty of the book of Revelation begins to explain some important facts about the kingdom of heaven on earth. The first of them is presented in a very graphic way. An angel comes from heaven with the key to the bottomless pit. He also has a great chain. He takes Satan and binds him for 1,000 years. He was cast into the bottomless pit for this period of time. The kingdom of Christ on earth will be a time when the intelligence behind evil will have no access to those on earth. There will be no temptation toward evil. No deception, no lies from the lips of demons.

While this coming kingdom has been prophesied many times over the centuries this is the first time the length of this glorious kingdom has been revealed.

While the exact length of the millennium is found only here however, the prophecies of the Old Testament imply the kingdom on earth will be for a long period of time. Isaiah said,

> "And it shall come to pass in that day, *that* the LORD shall punish the host of the high ones *that are* on high, and the kings of the earth upon the earth. And they shall be gathered together, *as* prisoners are gathered in the pit, and shall be shut up in the prison, and after many days shall they be visited. Then the moon shall be confounded, and the sun ashamed, when the LORD of hosts shall reign in mount Zion, and in Jerusalem, and before his ancients gloriously" (Isaiah 24:21-23).

The sequence of events in this Old Testament prophecy matches those in Revelation chapters 19 and 20. The time is not given in the exact number of years but indicates it will be for a long time.

The minor prophet Zechariah predicted the same scenario of events prior to the beginning of the thousand-year reign; the battle of Armageddon and Christ's coming to defeat the Gentile nations. Zechariah says Christ will touch down on the Mount of Olives at His coming. After describing the earthquake to take place the prophet announces the kingdom.

"And the LORD shall be king over all the earth: in that day shall there be one LORD, and his name one" (Zechariah 14:9).

The details about the kingdom of Christ on earth have been prophesied in many Old Testament passages. The Holy Spirit enabled those prophets to predict what Christ's kingdom would be like in that glad millennial day.

The prophet Isaiah gives insight as to the physical changes, the spiritual, moral and governmental changes in the day of Christ's reign on earth (Isaiah 11:1-6, 12:1-6; 35:1-10).

The following passage from Ezekiel may also be added to this list of references (Ezekiel 34:11-24). Ezekiel associates the re-gathering and restoration of Israel with the thousand-year reign of Christ on earth.

These partial references to Old Testament passages predicting the kingdom age show beyond question that Revelation 20 is not the only mention of the millennial kingdom, Christ's personal reign on earth.

Zechariah places the beginning of Christ reign over the nations of the world subsequence to His second coming. The book of Revelation follows the same sequence of these prophetic events as did the book of Zechariah.

Those Who Reign with Christ

The glorious second coming of Christ was prophesied by Enoch, the seventh from Adam. He said, "Behold, the Lord cometh with 10,000 of his saints." This is the first indication that when He returns the raptured church will be with Him.

The following passage from Revelation 1:5, 6, gives the same truth, "And from Jesus Christ, who is the faithful witness, and the first begotten of the dead, and the Prince of the kings of the earth. Unto him that loved us, and washed us from our sins in his own blood, and has made us kings and priests unto God and his father, to him be glory and dominion forever and ever. Amen."

"Behold he cometh with the clouds, and every eye shall see him."

The church is here designated as kings and priests unto God and this truth is given in the context of Christ's second coming.

Christ in His letter to the church of Laodicea promised the overcomers in that congregation they would be granted to sit with Him in his throne (Revelation 3:21).

When the twenty-four elders sang praise to Christ in the throne room of heaven after He had taken the sealed book form His Father's hands more light is given on the bride of Christ reigning with Him in His millennial kingdom. They sang, "Thou art worthy to take the book, and to open the seals thereof, for thou was slain and has redeemed us to God by thy blood out of every kindred, tongue, and people, and nation. And has made us unto our God kings and priests, and we shall reign on the Earth" (Revelation 5:9, 10).

The Bride of Christ Will Come Back with Christ and Reign with Him Here on Earth.

It would not be an exaggeration to say that a large number of modern-day Christians have not comprehended that reigning with Christ is in their future. The passage just considered declares it to be true. This concept is not just found in the book of Revelation. Paul wrote to Timothy, "If we suffer we shall also reign with him: If we deny him, he will also deny us." It is in our daily walk as believers, God is working into our experiences those spiritual qualities needed for reigning with Christ in the coming kingdom. It is in prayer and the bearing of affliction that we are prepared for a place at His side in the blessed millennial kingdom. But we who are His true disciples will reign with Christ is an eternal verity. For our souls sake we ought not to avoid this truth.

Paul Touched on This Doctrine in Writing to the Colossians

> "If ye then be risen with Christ, seek those things which are above, where Christ sitteth on the right hand of God. Set your affection on things above, not on things on the earth. For ye are dead, and your life is hid with Christ in God. When Christ, *who is* our life, shall appear, then shall ye also appear with him in glory" (Colossians 3:1-4).

If the future of Christians is to appear with Him in glory, this account in Revelation describes the glory "...they lived and reigned with Christ 1,000 years" (Revelation 20:46). What greater glory than the kingdom age when all the nations joyfully obey Christ's command and the righteous of the Lord will cover the earth as the waters cover the sea.

Matters of Resurrection

The resurrection becomes the subject of concern in verse five which states that the first resurrection is the rapture which takes place just before the great tribulation begins. The raptured church is the Bride of Christ who will return with Him to reign in the kingdom age. The Scripture says clearly that the rest of the dead will not be resurrected for 1,000 years. By the "rest of the dead" is meant those who died unsaved. They must also be resurrected to meet the Lord at the great white throne of judgment. It is important to note that the resurrection of the believers and the resurrection of the nonbelievers are both literal resurrection.

Settling this doctrine is essential to understanding the great white throne judgment.

The Final War

At the binding and imprisonment of Satan it was made known that by the end of the millennium he would be released from his imprisonment. Filled with anger he reacts very quickly by gathering a large army and takes up just where he left off when the angel bound him. Defeated in the war against God at the Armageddon the devil immediately directs his military power against the people of God in the city of God.

Without delay God Almighty sends fire out of heaven and destroys Satan's forces. God then cast Satan into "the lake of fire and brimstone to be tormented day and night forever and ever."

The Great White Throne of Judgment

This incredible chapter comes to a close with a brief account of the resurrection and the judgment of the wicked. The face of Him who sat on the throne so displayed the glory of God that the earth and heaven fled away. This judgment is consistent with the absolute perfection and holiness of God within the parameters of mercy, justice and truth. There will be no mistakes or injustices at the Great White Throne. Every person will be judged according to their works. The absence of their name from the book of life determines their place where the devil, the demons, the beast and the false prophet have already been placed. It is the place prepared for the devil and his angels. Jesus taught, the resurrected wicked will have only eternal damnation ahead of them.

CHAPTER
FOURTEEN

A Glimpse at Eternity

Revelation 21 and 22

The consideration of time and space history has come to an end and the two remaining chapters deal only with matters relating to eternity. This conclusion rests on verse one which says, "And I saw a new earth; for the first heaven and the first earth were passed away, and there was no more sea."

John's recent visions had shown that all the saved were safely with the Lord, all the unsaved were in the Lake of Fire. Satan and his demonic forces were all in the Lake of Fire as well. The first heaven and the first earth were gone, or as Peter describes it "the elements melted with the fervent heat." Everything related to time is finished.

With this vision John is introduced to everything new. The new heaven, a new earth, and a new city, a new people yet there is a familiar ring to these words. New does not mean strange or foreign. It means the familiar has been made eternally holy by the powerful righteous and creative hand of Almighty God. John noticed that there was no more sea. Expositors have made many efforts to explain this statement without success. The Scripture merely states the fact that there is no sea in the new world and no explanation is given for its absence.

John next saw the holy city, New Jerusalem, descending from heaven. The beauty of the city was incredible for it was adorned as a bride for her husband. This is not a symbolic city but a real city. Its connection with the Bride of Christ will be considered later in this chapter.

The scene was followed by a voice from heaven explaining that God is now dwelling with man and they should be His people. God declares He will be the God of this new people. His personal care will allay their fears; comfort them with the glorious truth that all the distresses of life in the first world are gone forever. Death is replaced by immortality in eternity.

The truth becomes clear in verse five that though the thousand-year reign of Christ is now over the kingdom of God and the Lamb has become the eternal king. The kingdom is eternal. From His throne the king of eternity declares, "Behold I make all things new." John was then instructed to offer in his writing the truth uttered by Christ from the throne. He also was to write that Christ's words are always faithful and that is a promise that will hold good for all eternity.

He that sat upon the throne identifies himself as Alpha and Omega, the beginning and the end. This can be none other than the eternal Christ. It is He that came as Redeemer in the first world and opened the fountain of the waters of life. His promise to the overcomer is the inheritance of all things and the assurance that He will be their God and they will be His sons.

The Lord declares from the throne that the wicked of every kind has been dealt with and consigned eternally to the Lake of Fire.

The New Jerusalem, the Lamb's Wife

One of the angels which poured out the bowls of the wrath of God comes to John asking him to follow that he might show him the Bride, the Lamb's wife. Previously an angel took John into the wilderness to show him the Scarlet woman seated on the beast (Revelation 17:1). Now in this vision John has the privilege of seeing the Bride with Christ who is the moral antithesis of the Scarlet woman, known as the great whore. Purity, modesty and holiness characterize the Lamb's Bride.

John was then transported in the spirit to a high mountain from which he had a good view of the great, holy Jerusalem, coming down out of heaven. The city is said to have the glory of God the features of which are given in the next sixteen verses of this chapter.

Such an actual city has been anticipated by the godly since the days of Abraham. The writer of Hebrews says that the ancient patriarchs looked for a city which had foundation whose Builder and Maker was God (Hebrews 11:10). Verse sixteen of the eleventh chapter of the book of Hebrews says, "Wherefore God is not ashamed to be called their God; for he hath prepared for them a city" (Hebrews 11:16). Later in the book of Hebrews mention is made once again of this anticipated city.

> "But ye are come to Mount Zion and unto the city of the living god, and to an innumerable company of angels. To the general assembly and church of the firstborn, which are written in heaven, and to God the Judge of all, and to the spirits of just men made perfect" (Hebrews 12:22,23).

Hebrews makes one more significant statement about the city. "For here we have no continuing city, but we seek one to come" (Hebrews 13:14).

There can be no doubt that the city John saw in this vision is the city toward which the saints on earth have been journeying across the ages.

John calls the city the Lamb's Wife. Some contend that this argues against the New Jerusalem being a literal city. But the reality is this magnificent metropolis is the eternal home of the Bride of Christ. Revelation 21:27 states that the population of this city is made up exclusively of those whose names are written in the Lamb's book of life.

It is true that the major features of this holy city give a symbolic picture of the moral and spiritual perfections of the Lamb's Bride.

The impressive wall of the New Jerusalem rest on twelve huge foundation stones, inscribed with the names of the twelve apostles. The Bride who dwells here has been saved by faith in the foundation of truth laid by the apostles under the direction of Christ.

Christ told the disciples that long ago night in the upper room that He was returning to the Father's house to build a place for them. He did return and build a home for all the ransomed Church of God.

John learned that this New Jerusalem had no temple. None was needed for God the Father and God the Son are the Temple. This feature again speaks of the Bride. In her earthly journey she had learned that true worship was not a matter of building and altars but direct and personal fellowship with God himself.

New Jerusalem has no natural source of light. God, the Father, Son and Holy Spirit generate all the light that will ever be needed in the world to come. The light calls attention to the bride who lives in the new city. In her days on earth Jesus said of her, "Ye are the light of the world."

While John looks on, the Angel measured the city walls and gates. He found it to be an enormous cube 1500 miles wide, 1500 miles long of 1500 miles high. It easily transcends the most elaborate and magnificent structure ever built on earth. The carpenter from Nazareth died, rose from the dead, ascended to heaven and in His glorified state built for His Bride the holy Jerusalem. If you are truly a Christian this is where you will live forever.

Before we leave this chapter, consideration needs to be given to who will populate the New Jerusalem and the new earth. It has already been established that the church, the Bride of Christ, will live in the New Jerusalem. All those who have died, righteous and been resurrected from the deal will also inhabit the holy city. That would mean the Old Testament saints and the tribulation saints will take up residence in this remarkable city.

Who then will populate the new earth? Revelation 21:3 speaks of the new people among which God will dwell in the eternal age. They will be His people and He will be their God.

Revelation 21:23-24 says that God will be the light of the new city and that the nations of them which are saved shall walk in the light of the holy city. The kings of the earth will bring their glory and honor into it. Verse 26 says they will also bring the glory and honor of the nations into the New Jerusalem.

A great many expositors of Revelation believe that the holy city will hover over the earth during the millennium and the nations shall walk in its light. The difficulty with this interpretation is the lack of any statement that this was in God's plan. It is therefore an assumption lacking other scriptural support. This position also overlooks the reality of the human population on the new earth. A population that have been saved out of history past and so transformed by the grace of God that they are both sinless and perfect as are all the saints living in the holy city.

To deny the existence of nations in the eternal age is countered by the fact that the nations are mentioned three times in two chapters on eternity (Revelation 21;24, 26; 22;2). The kings of the earth are spoken of in Revelation 21:24. To arbitrarily transfer these passages to the millennium is a violation of this text.

So there will be people and nations on the new earth. Where will this human population come from? For a start let us consider God's already revealed plans for the covenant nation. Twice in the prophecy of Isaiah the future of Israel is related to the new heaven and the new earth. Isaiah prophesied, "For behold, I create new heavens and a new earth, and the former shall not be remembered, nor come into mind" (Isaiah 65:17). The remainder of the 65th chapter is related to millennial days. The prophet relates Israel to the new heaven and a new earth.

J. Dwight Pentecost wrote the following regarding Israel and the new earth, "Israel's covenant guarantees that the people, the land, a national existence, a kingdom, a king, and spiritual blessings in perpetuity" (Things to Come, Dunham Publishing Company, 1961, page 561).

In Isaiah 66:22 it is written, "For as the new heavens and the new earth, which I will make, shall remain before me, saith the Lord so shall your seed and your name remain." From these passages is evident that Israel will exist as a nation in the eternal new earth.

There must be other nations for the word "nation" in the plural form is found three times in Revelation 21 and 22. After Christ's second coming, Matthew records that He will sit upon the throne of His glory and before Him will be gathered all the nations to be judged. The sheep nations were put at His right hand the goat nations on the left. To those on His right hand Christ said, "Come ye blessed of my father, inherit the kingdom prepared for you from the foundation of the world" (Matthew 25:34). To the goat nations He said, "Depart from me, ye cursed, into everlasting fire, prepared for the devil and his angels."

The sheep nations demonstrated their faithfulness and their relationship to Israel on earth. They like Israel restored will enter the eternal kingdom. They are no longer Gentile nations but "sheep" nations for they follow the Great Shepherd of the sheep our Lord Jesus Christ. These godly people will with Israel populate the new earth. The Bible does not indicate that they will reproduce in the new Earth. It would seem that this population will remain the same in numbers throughout eternity. There is no mention made of either death or reproduction in the eternal age.

We can now account for the earthly population of the new Earth and the population of the New Jerusalem. All will be godly, pure of heart, righteous in conduct. The entire population will forever enjoy true spirituality in the immediate presence of the Father and the Son.

Chapter 22 takes up another important aspect of life in the new Earth. John is now inside the holy city. He is shown the stream of pure water flowing out of the throne of God and the Lamb producing a river flowing down by a street. On each side of the river is the tree of life. Monthly it bears twelve different kinds of fruit. The leaves from the tree of life were intended for the healing of the nations. What need for healing could there possibly be on the new earth? The answer is found in the Greek word translated healing. It also means preventive healing. Evidently it gives the body all it needs to keep well.

This account cannot help but bring to the reader's mind the Garden of Eden, man's original home at creation. At the end of time and the beginning of eternity God created an eternal home for the saved that has everything in it God ever intended should be in the original Garden of Eden had it not been for sin. By the perfect redemptive work of Christ sin has been removed forever from the home of the blood bought souls living in the new earth and its holy city New Jerusalem. It will be their privilege to feed on the fruit and leaves of the tree of life. The curse that rested on the first earth is gone and none can ever come on the new earth.

In verse three we learn that the throne of God and the Lamb is in the city. Therefore, the government of the new Earth is the eternal kingdom of God. There will be no inactivity there for His servants will joyfully serve Him constantly.

The most exciting phrase in this chapter is "they shall see his face" (verse four). What glory, what great expectation to live day by day seeing His face. Each person will have His name on their foreheads.

There will be no night in the new earth. It will be broad daylight all the time. There will be plenty for saints to do. We've already noted they will serve Christ and they who ruled with Christ during the millennium will continue to reign in the eternal age.

In verse six the angel told John that what he had heard is faithful and true. It is the Lord God of the holy prophets who arranged through His angels that those who serve Him might know what will shortly come to pass. What a strong emphasis is placed on prophecy by the above statement. Prophecy is not a sideline in the purpose of God. Prophecy is mainstream and keeps the child of God in touch with the way that God works in the affairs of this world. For the enlightened Christians it is foolhardy to ignore what God has shared with us about His plans for the kingdom.

At the beginning of the book of Revelation Christ said those who read the book will be blessed. In this last chapter of Revelation He says very forthrightly, "Behold I come quickly," keep the truth expounded in this book and you will be blessed. Christ expects us to be aware of the prophetic truth in the Word. Since His coming is imminent it should be a daily concern for the child of God.

John once again succumbs to the urge to worship the angel and was rebuked for his action and exhorted to worship God. The angel's final word to John was the instruction to leave the book of Revelation unsealed. The practical reason is that the time is at hand.

To explain the point the angel said," He that is unjust, let him be unjust still; and he which is filthy, let him be filthy still; and he that is righteous, let him be righteous still; and he that is holy, let him be holy still" (Revelation 22:11).

In view of the imminent coming of Christ, meaning He could come any time of the day or night, are you ready to meet Him in the air or would you be left unready for His coming?

He brings the reader face-to-face with the possibility of being frozen, figuratively speaking, in your present spiritual condition forever. There is nothing like prophetic truth to bring the soul to the hour of decision.

The remainder of this final chapter is a moving admonition to all who read the book to take seriously the wonderful unveiling of the Lord Jesus Christ in His full power and glory and the fact that He will impact this world like nothing else has ever been done.

He will by His own will overrule all human endeavor and opposition to close history and shut the door on this present world so He may open the door on eternity, the Paradise of God, the home of the redeemed forever.

The closing verses of chapter 22 are addressed to the individual believer and also to the church as a corporate body. The final beatitude defines who has the right to enter the holy city. Only they that do Christ's commandments may dwell in the city and eat form the tree of life. This indicates the fact that those who believe savingly in Jesus Christ are called to the way of obedience. This truth has fallen through the cracks with the church of our day.

Verse fifteen interrupts the series of admonitions to point out the final separation that divides those in Christ eternal kingdom form those who are without because they believed not.

Jesus spoke to John emphasizing the importance of the message His angel has given the church in this book of Revelation. They remind the old apostle of when Jesus lived on earth and taught the disciples of His majestic offices. Jesus is from the line of David speaking of His kingly office. He is also "the bright and morning Star." In this title is the victory of the eternal Christ, He is light for all people for all eternity. He is the light of His body here on earth leading her on as the lights go out in this fallen world. What great incentive to long for and ready oneself for the meeting in the air the day of the rapture.

The Last Call for Sinners to Come to Christ

The Holy Spirit will be empowering the church to present the gospel of the Lord Jesus Christ right down to the final hour. The Spirit will continue to convict and convince the sinner of his need and to cultivate a thirst for God in the hearts of unbelievers. The Lord Jesus is in these words asking the church to remain faithful in her testimony with a day by day life of practical holiness.

The last warning in the Bible (Revelation 22:18-19) underscores the truth that the Scriptures are inspired of the Holy Spirit, inerrant, infallible, incorruptible and the final authority. Put simply, these verses are saying be careful what you do with God's precious Word. Your eternity depends on it.

The last book of the Bible closes with a prayer. It is short but oh so significant. Jesus' last words to John the Revelator were, "Surely I come quickly." John, with holy and humble affirmation, cries out, "Amen, even so, come Lord Jesus."

The last benediction of the Bible is full of comfort. "The grace of our Lord Jesus Christ be with you all. Amen."

CHAPTER
FIFTEEN

Prophecy for the Soul

The last book of the Bible does more than inform believers of the fulfillment of prophecy in the last days. Such knowledge brings to the reader's attention deep soul transforming issues that need to be dealt with. Sprinkled through the book of Revelation are seven beatitudes rich in devotional and spiritual insights. When Jesus preached the Sermon on the Mount He introduced the principles of the kingdom of heaven with a series of beatitudes. Now the glorified Christ having given His church a picture of the close of history and the onset of eternity presents believers with seven more beatitudes to show them the pathway of personal blessing to be found in the study of Bible prophecy.

The study of Bible prophecy should never be merely academic. When we allow the Spirit to guide and teach us it becomes a personal encounter with the living Christ and such an encounter with revealed truth cannot but change us spiritually. The study of Revelation is not complete until we have discovered in these seven beatitudes Christ's special message to our hearts as we wait for His coming.

A. B. Simpson once spoke of Revelation as God's last word to His people in the present dispensation. There could be no greater reason for getting serious about the Revelation of Jesus Christ than that. What a treasure of grace and goodness are these gems of truth that call our attention to obedience.

The First Beatitude

The first beatitude is in the prologue of chapter one. "Blessed is he that readeth, and they that hear the words of this prophecy, and keep those things that are written therein; for the time is at hand" (Revelation 1:3). The Greek word translated read actually means to read aloud. The Lord Jesus expects that Revelation will be part of our personal reading but that it should also be read to the gathered church. Believers are urged to keep the word and that is only possible when we read the word and hear it read. The implication of this beatitude is reading this book and for that matter all inspired scripture will put demands on one's soul. The last phrase, "for the time is at hand," connects this spiritual exercise to the glorious doctrine of the imminent return of Jesus Christ.

The Second Beatitude

The second beatitude in Revelation is found in chapter fourteen and the verse thirteen an angel has just declared the everlasting gospel warning earth-dwellers of the impending judgment. A voice from heaven speaks, "Write, blessed are the dead which die in the Lord from henceforth: Yea saith the Spirit, that they may rest from their labours: and their works do follow them" (Revelation 14:13).

This message comes in one of the darkest hours of human history. A voice from heaven encourages the tribulation saints that it is blessed to die in the Lord for they shall rest from all their labours. An added blessing is that their works will follow them. This truth is not only for tribulation saints but for all who die in the Lord. This beatitude makes death for the child of God an incredible blessing. He loses nothing for his works follow him. One must ask the question, "How much of what I am doing is worth taking on to glory?" It is only what we do for Christ that will be worthy in that day.

The Third Beatitude

The next beatitude is given in the description of Satan's strategy to bring the nations of the world to the battle of Armageddon. Christ breaks into the flow of this dreadful scene with an explanation of His personal role in all this. He says, "Behold, I come as a thief." He uses this metaphor to make plain the manner of His coming. Christ is to come suddenly and unannounced. It is evident from the language of this beatitude that Christ is speaking to all who wait for His coming.

> "Blessed is he that watcheth, and keepeth his garments, lest he walk naked, and they see his shame" (Revelation 16:15).

This beatitude addresses the issue of our personal readiness for Christ's return. We should be actively watching for His coming and have on the garment appropriate for His coming. It is to be a wedding garment. The first phase of His return is His descent into the air and the catching away of the church, His bride, to meet Him in the air. The garment is important for it is a testimony of our total commitment to Christ. To neglect these spiritual obligations is to bring shame up on ourselves and upon our Lord. Are we consistently ready to meet Him?

The Fourth Beatitude

The background of the fourth beatitude is different in that it is given in a heavenly scene. John said,

> "I heard as it were the voice of a great multitude, and the voice of many waters, and a voice of mighty thundering, saying; Alleluia for the Lord God omnipotent reigneth. Let us be glad and rejoice and give honor to him; for the marriage of the Lamb is come, and his wife has made herself ready," (Revelation 19:6,7).

John is then given the beatitude and told to write it.

> "Blessed are they which are called to the marriage supper of the Lamb," (Revelation 19:9).

The call in this beatitude is the gospel call. It is a call to renounce sin and everything of the old life and become part of the bride of Christ. Paul no doubt had this beatitude in mind when he wrote to the Corinthians, "For I have espoused you to one husband, that I may present you as a chaste virgin to Christ," (2 Corinthians 11:12).

A word was added to this beatitude that should not be overlooked. John was told, "These are the true sayings of God." The beatitude is inspired scripture and therefore authoritative. We are assured of their fulfillment.

The Fifth Beatitude

It is in the chapter on the millennium that the fifth beatitude is found.

> "Blessed and holy is he that hath part in the first resurrection; on such the second death has no power, but they shall be priests of God and of Christ, and shall reign with him a thousand years," (Revelation 20:6).

The first resurrection has reference to the rapture of the church described in First Thessalonians 4:14-18. This beatitude declares that the raptured church will actually reign with Christ on earth for the duration of the millennium. The raptured saints will have no fear of the second death that will come on the wicked at the Great White Throne judgment. The bride of Christ will be with the Lord Jesus enjoying the blessings of eternity forever.

The expectations this beatitude presents for the believer are worthy of our frequent meditation and study. The consideration of these eternal prospects nurtures the soul and move us toward the blessed state of Christlikeness. A growing understanding of how our lives are related to Bible prophecy should be a normal part of the process of spiritual maturation.

The Sixth Beatitude

While John the apostle was touring the inside of the holy city, New Jerusalem, he was told by the angel,

> "And he said unto me, these sayings are faithful and true: and the Lord God of the holy prophets sent his angels to show unto his servants the things which must shortly come to pass. Behold, I come quickly, blessed is he

that keepeth the sayings of the prophecy of this book," (Revelation 22:6,7).

The language of this beatitude echoes the message of the first beatitude in Revelation 1:3. The truths of Revelation are to be guarded and carried out. This would imply that the believer is held accountable for the manner in which he applies these truths in his daily walk. The beatitudes of this book make prophecy both practical and personal. The imminence of Christ is never lost sight of in the seven beatitudes. If the imminence of Jesus' return is treated with indifference the soul will suffer the loss of a very strong motivation to holiness.

The Seventh Beatitude

When the final beatitude is given, John is still taking in the glory of the holy city. He is careful to record that the source of the beautiful river is the throne of God. John shortly makes a second reference to the throne in verse three.

"And there shall be no more curse: but the throne of God and the Lamb shall be in it; and his servants shall serve Him," (Revelation 22:3).

These mentions of the throne of God and the Lamb verify that the kingdom of God will be the authority in eternity. As Isaiah said of Christ, the government shall be upon His shoulders for all the countless ages of eternity. The verse declares that no force can ever alter His glorious reign. These verses are the context for beatitude number seven.

Christ Himself speaks, "And behold I come quickly; and my reward is with me, to give every man according as his word shall be, I am Alpha and Omega, the beginning and the end, the first and the last."

The last beatitude is then given.

"Blessed are they that do his commandments, that they may have right to the tree of life, and may enter in through the gates into the city," (Revelation 22:14).

Christian obedience is the main issue in the final beatitude in Revelation. It reminds us of Jesus' words when He instructed the apostles about making disciples and baptizing them. Jesus taught that as soon as they were baptized they were to be "taught to observe all things whatsoever he commanded them" (Matthew 28:19,20). Obedience does not save us, but we are saved to obey Him.

Standing with John on the edge of eternity we are reminded that obedience has eternal reward. The Lord Jesus has reserved for His obedient children the right to the tree of life and the key to the gates of the New Jerusalem.

Western culture has rebelled against God and it is not an exaggeration to say that much of the professing church has forgotten the long ago call to obedience our Savior made while He was still here on earth. He is still saying from the throne room in heaven, "Blessed are they that do His commandments." Obedience is not radical Christianity. It is normal Christianity.

Appendices

Throughout this study of the Book of Revelation doctrinal themes have emerged that deserve some serious consideration. The appendices have been written to provide a more in-depth consideration of some of the theological issues than the text would allow. These are not complete or exhaustive studies of any of these subjects but will assist the reader in seeing the importance of these truths.

These appendices are intended to help those searching for answers about the end-time and the place these issues have in the fulfillment of Bible prophecy. They are designed to help us in discovering how to live Christ-like in a world where the sun is going down on human history. In prophecy we learn that in a world where the sun's going down, God is announcing another sunrise.

"But unto you that fear, my name shall the Sun of Righteousness arises with healing in his wings; and ye shall go forth and grow up as calves in the stall" (Malachi 4:2). This Old Testament prophecy of the Second Coming of Christ clearly announces the dawn of an eternal day.

Appendix A

Revelation and the Kingdom

The grand theme of the book of Revelation is Jesus Christ Himself bringing redemptive history to its close. He does so in His office as king. He is king of kings, Lord of Lords, the king of eternity and the Blessed and only Potentate. As Christ will come out of heaven mounted on a white horse, there will be many crowns on his head. The scripture says inscribed in his vesture will be the words "King of Kings and Lord of Lords."

Why this crown and the regal name? The scriptures prophesy that Christ will rule the nations. He has not yet carried out this office. It will only be when Christ Jesus returns to earth again that He will extend His rule over the entire world. The church's prayer, "Thy kingdom come, thy will be done, in earth as it is in Heaven" will then be answered. Nothing but a literal, divine government administered by the Lord Jesus Christ right here on earth can answer that prayer.

The twentieth chapter of Revelation puts the kingdom age after Christ's Second Coming. No one else can bring in the kingdom. It is not the work of the church. The kingdom of God during the church age is not publicly manifest. The present aspect of the kingdom is an inner heart experience. Jesus told Nicodemus he must be born again both to understand the kingdom and to enter the kingdom.

Jesus said to His followers, "Fear not, little flock, it is your Father's good pleasure to give you the kingdom" (Luke 12:32). It is in the future when the raptured church returns with Christ to earth that this promise is fulfilled.

Many churches and individual Christians have been led to believe that the church must work hard and pray in the kingdom. For two thousand years, that approach has been a failure. It has failed because it is not sound doctrine. The church has not been called to fix up the world and establish the kingdom. The church is to evangelize the nations of the world and wait patiently for Christ's return when He will personally set up the kingdom of God on earth.

The scripture teaches that the redeemed church will reign with Christ in the wondrous kingdom age. Revelation 5:10 teaches that the blood-washed church will be made kings and priests unto God. That promise carries through to Revelation 20 where it is reworded, "They shall be priests of God and of Christ and shall reign with Him a thousand years." It is also stated that this reign with Christ will be on earth (Revelation 5:9,10).

Another enlightening reference to the reign of believers is found in the letter Christ sent to the church in Thyatira. It is a very specific promise to those who by the grace of God are overcomers. Christ says, "He that overcometh and keepeth my works unto the end, to him will I give power over the nations." The Greek word used for power here means "to be given authority." The scripture teaches that the church saints will be rulers with Christ during the thousand year reign.

The millennial reign will make universal peace and universal righteousness the social order of the day. The question has been raised as to an age where righteousness will be enforced. All who govern and all who instruct and teach will be fully redeemed and therefore sinless and perfect. All the influences upon mankind will be good. Satan and his demons will be totally removed from the scene rendering them unable to tempt men to sin and disobey. Righteous behavior will prevail during these thousand years.

At the end of the kingdom age Satan will be released and immediately begin his deceptive recruiting of men to follow him as he opposes Christ's kingdom. This circumstance indicates that during the millennium, righteousness prevailed. But with the introduction of Satan those whose hearts were not transformed during the millennium will follow Satan without hesitation. This gives evidence that people cannot be forced to righteousness. Some will show outward expressions of right living but they will not be converted. Vast numbers of souls will be saved during Christ's literal reign over the nations. They will be saved by faith in the finished work of Christ resulting in their resurrection. Salvation has only been by faith in every age of redemptive history.

There are those among the liberal theologians who attack the concept of the kingdom with a sovereign king on the throne. They believe the idea of throne and righteousness are antiquated ideas irrelevant to the modern world. They contend the democratic government by the people is the answer. The Bible reveals that that kingdom is a concept that comes from God and will be the only form of government to survive at the end of history. The eternal age will have only the kingdom of God and Jesus Christ will be sitting on the throne of that blessed and holy government.

We who follow Christ as the Sovereign now and look for His return and subsequent reign gladly surrender to His Lordship. It is the issue of surrender that bothers the liberals. They fail to study the government of heaven and the new earth. For the Christians, the sovereign rule of Jesus Christ is one of the brightest spots in eternity. If we have known the delight and blessing of that rule in our hearts we will find living in His kingdom to be joy unspeakable and fully glory.

There are a number of reasons why the last days of human history should be lived out in the millennial kingdom. The first is Christological reason. The New Testament scriptures show that Christ is king of kings and will rule the nations with a rod of iron. These privileges He has not exercised but He will during the thousand year reign. A second reason for such a kingdom is found in the unconditional promise given to Abraham. The patriarch was promised an area of land reaching from the river of Egypt to the Mesopotamia north. Neither Abraham nor his descendants have ever possessed fully that geographical territory. During the millennium, Israel with be both physically and literally restored as the covenant nation. They will be participants in the millennial rule and will realize at that time the full land God covenanted to them.

A third reason is that it demonstrates that Jesus Christ has made full atonement for all sin. The effects of such a full salvation will be the universal righteousness that will prevail during the thousand year reign.

Interestingly, Revelation chapter twenty necessitates clear thinking as to the hermeneutics employed. Is the passage symbolic or allegorical? Or is this scripture to be taken literally? Those who reject the idea of the millennial kingdom do so on the grounds that the passage should be spiritualized. The narrative is seen as depicting some aspect of the church. The context is ignored. That the passage is part of Revelation that is dealing with the future has been overlooked.

The first rule of hermeneutics is to take the passage literally unless there is clear evidence to do otherwise. Taking this chapter literally is the first step toward understanding it.

The persons and actions in this chapter are consistent with other facts in Revelation and with kingdom concepts found elsewhere in the Bible. It is speaking of an actual kingdom on earth ruled by Christ and His church. The time of the kingdom is clearly defined. It lies between the resurrection of the righteous and the resurrection of the wicked. The duration of the kingdom is clearly spelled out. Revelation twenty is a straightforward prophecy of the kingdom age that fits other kingdom teaching in both the Old Testament and New Testament.

Appendix B

Revelation and the Rapture

The word rapture is not found in the book of Revelation nor is it in any other book of the Bible. Rapture is from a Latin root and basically means caught away or snatched away. It has long been the popular term for the resurrection of the righteous dead and the translation of the living believers at Christ's coming for His bride, the church.

The best plan for studying the rapture is to examine the scripture passages from which this doctrine is derived. The first mention of this truth took place in the upper room the night before Jesus was crucified. The Lord Jesus told His troubled disciples that He was going to the Father and there He would prepare a place for them. Jesus then promised them, "I will come again, and receive you unto myself; that where I am. There ye may be also." This is the first announcement that Jesus would come personally to receive His church. John 14:1-3 is step one in learning about the rapture.

In Paul's first letter to the church at Thessalonica mention is made of the rapture. Paul wrote,

> "For the Lord himself shall descend from heaven with a shout, and the voice of the archangel, and with the trumpet of God: and the dead in Christ shall rise first: Then we which are alive shall be caught up together with them in the clouds to meet the Lord in the air: And so shall we ever be with the Lord" (I Thessalonians 4:16,17).

It is here that we learn that Christ's Second Coming will be in two phases. He will first come in the air to meet His church and rapture her to heaven. His Second Coming to the earth will take place after the Great Tribulation. Zechariah tells us He will touch down on the Mount of Olives. This event will be visible to the whole world as Christ descends mounted on a white horse and followed by the armies of heaven made up of the church saints (Revelation 19:11-16).

In Paul's letter to the Philippian congregation he discloses some more truth about the rapture. He told the church, "For our conversation is in heaven; from whence also we look for the Saviour, the Lord Jesus Christ: Who shall change our vile body, that it may be fashioned like unto his glorious body. According to the working whereby he is able even to subdue all things unto himself" (Philippians 3:20, 21). The rapture in this passage is described as a radical change in our bodies. For the dead believers their bodies will be resurrected and for the living believers their bodies will be changed to immortal bodies by the power of the risen Christ.

The rapture is a divine work that will fashion our bodies after the risen body of the Lord Jesus. What an incredible blessing this change will bring to the believer and what possibilities it will introduce in the life of the believer in eternity.

Paul's great chapter on the resurrection has a section that throws light on how the change will take place and the results of such a dynamic change. I Corinthians 15:50 opens the passage with these words, "Now this I say, brethren, flesh and blood cannot inherit the kingdom of God; neither doth corruption inherit incorruption." Paul explains theologically why the rapture is necessary. To inherit the kingdom the believer must undergo this supernatural transformation that makes his body like Christ's resurrection body. The apostle calls this wonderful work of God a mystery. The mystery is that we shall not all die but we will all be changed at the time of the rapture.

The next two verses provide a very short but profound explanation of the event we call the rapture. It is instantaneous, taking only a moment, the twinkling of an eye. It takes place exactly at the sound of the trumpet. The dead believers will be raised and the living believers will be changed. The impact of the rapture will make both the dead and the living saints incorruptible and immortal.

Nothing is said about the rapture being a public event. The meeting of Christ and His bride in the air will be secret but it will not be unnoticed for the disappearance of people of all ages and races across the world in multiplied millions will have an impact on every aspect of life on earth.

Having defined the rapture Biblically the next step is to determine the time of the rapture. This is a favorite battleground among prophecy preachers and writers. A remarkable selection of ideas has been spawned over the years. The following are the best known of the theories for the time of the rapture.

A. The Pre-tribulation Rapture
B. The Pre-wrath Rapture
C. The Mid-tribulation Rapture
D. The Post-tribulation Rapture

It is evident that all four of these positions have an effect on the interpretation of the book of Revelation. I recently read a book by an evangelical writer who gave all four theories and suggested that the reader solve the matter as to which is right. Multiple choice is not a principle of Biblical hermeneutics. The truth is each theory will have its own substantial effect on the interpretation of the book of Revelation. After some fifty years in the study of Revelation and after serious study of the above positions on the timing of the rapture I have come to believe that the pre-tribulation rapture position is the one that fits the inherent structure of the book of Revelation. This book has been written with that in mind.

There are three Pauline messages that indicate a pre-tribulation rapture. In I Thessalonians 1:9,10, the apostle commends this group of new Christians for waiting for God's Son from heaven. They were taking the doctrine of the Second Coming of Christ as personal and very important to them. Paul also reminds them that they have been saved from the wrath to come. Why should they even think about having to go through any portion of the wrath of God for they have been saved from that wrath. The tribulation is the wrath of the Lamb and the church saints have been delivered from that. The church will therefore be raptured prior to the beginning of the tribulation.

Paul's second epistle to the Thessalonians has a reference to the coming of the antichrist on the prophetic scene. He says that the antichrist cannot appear until the restrainer is removed. In II Thessalonians 2:6,7 the restrainer is mentioned twice, once as a neuter and the second time as masculine. The Holy Spirit is the force that has the power to restrain the level of evil in this world. The neuter is the church indwelt by the Holy Spirit. Christ called the church the salt of the earth. He was speaking not of Christendom but the true pilgrim church. Were it not for the presence of the Holy Spirit indwelt church still on earth the flood tides of evil would overpower the world as it will do in the days of the tribulation. This is a strong argument for the pre-tribulation rapture.

Paul's third passage on this subject is found in I Thessalonians 5:9,10. He pictures the believers as those who are awake and fully aware of the imminent coming of Christ. They do not sleep but are sober and watching for His coming which could occur at any time. The close of this chapter is so edifying as he says, "For God has not appointed us to wrath, but to obtain salvation by our Lord Jesus Christ, who died for us that whether we wake or sleep, we shall live together with him."

From the above scriptures it is obvious that the expectation of the rapture was common before the Revelation was ever written. When we come to the Revelation no mention is ever made of that event. The book begins with the church very much in view. John beholds the glorified Christ standing in the midst of the church here on earth. Chapters two and three are made up of an overall view of the church from Pentecost to the rapture. Chapter four makes a radical change. John is taken up unto heaven and finds himself in the throne room of God. There he finds the raptured church worshipping the Lamb of God. Not a word is said about the rapture but the result of the rapture is fully evident. John sees the church in heaven before the tribulation begins.

Appendix C

Revelation and Pre-Millennialism

It is obvious that this study of Revelation is written from the Pre-millennial position. While there are other interpretations of the 20th chapter of the book of Revelation, Pre-millennialism is consistent with the scripture text and its context. The facts are that John's vision of this section predicts the personal and public return of Christ just prior to the thousand year reign. Christ has defeated all His enemies and proceeds to establish His kingdom. There is nothing in the text that would suggest that this kingdom is symbolical or that it will be located anywhere else but on planet earth. The scripture states time boundaries during which the reign will take place. It lies between the resurrection of the righteous and the resurrection of the wicked. No one but Christ can establish this kingdom. It must await His Second Coming. It also fits the pattern of the prophecies of the Old Testament with regard to Messiah's kingdom.

The First Century Church was Pre-Millennial

There have been preserved letters and books written during the early church which allow us to know how the first Christians understood Revelation 20. The evidence is clear that the first century church was Pre-millennial and that position prevailed well into the fourth century.

Barnabas

This early church father wrote an epistle that makes reference to the millennium. His understanding was that God made the whole creation in six days and that the history of man would last for six thousand years after which there would be a Sabbatical millennium. He associates this thousand years with the coming of God's Son. Wickedness will be overcome and righteousness will prevail during the thousand years rest (The Ante-Nicene Fathers Vol. I, The Epistle of Barnabas, Chapter XV, pages 146, 147).

Papias

Papias was very early and knew the apostle John so he had direct contact with the apostles of Christ. Much of his writing was destroyed in a fire but copies were later located in Latin so some of his significant statements on the millennium were preserved. One quote from the existing fragments say, "… that there will be a millennium after the resurrection from the dead, when the personal reign of Christ will be established on earth," (Ante-Nicene Fathers, Vol. I, Fragments of Papias, page 154).

Polycarp

In his Epistle to the Philippians, he speaks of the millennium in chapter V, "True believers will be resurrected from the dead and reign with Christ. He warns that those who do evil will not inherit the kingdom of God," (Ante-Nicene Fathers, Vol. I, page 34).

Justin Martyr

One of the most informative early church writers on the doctrine of the millennium was Justin Martyr. He wrote more on this subject than most of the fathers. His epistle to Trypo the Jew contains an extensive treatment of Bible prophecy. He carefully explains to Trypo how Christ as His Second Coming will establish His kingdom. He says of the millennium, "In His days shall righteousness flourish, and abundance of peace until the moon be taken away. He shall have dominion from sea to sea and from the rivers to the end of the earth," (Ante-Nicene Fathers, Vol. I, The Epistle of Trypo, pages 209-211).

Irenaeus

Irenaeus, the Bishop of Lyons, was a strong Pre-millenarian. In his work entitled "Irenaeus Against Heresies," he gives a clear picture of the early church's understanding of the millennium. Chapter XXXIII is an extensive study of the times of the kingdom. Using the Old Testament prophets he shows what conditions will exist on earth during this kingdom. He clearly spells out the place of the resurrected church saints as ruling with Christ (Ante-Nicene Fathers, Vol. I, Irenaeus Against Heresies, pages 562-567).

Another valuable source for information on the writings of the church fathers on the millennium is George N.H. Peters. His work called "The Theocratic Kingdom" lists many quotes from the early Christian writers.

His quote from the History of Eusebius confirms the strong Pre-millenarian stand of the early church.

"Eusebius states that it had been the prevailing doctrine in the church and that until the early part of the third century it was held by most and questioned by none whose names have been preserved... So far as the question in reference to the sure and certain hope, entertained by the Christian world that the Redeemer would appear on earth, and the exercise authority during a thousand years. There is a good ground for the assertion of Mede, Dowel and Burnet and other writers on the same side, that down to the beginning of the fourth century the belief was universal and undisputed," (George N.H. Peters, The Theocratic Kingdom, Vol, I, footnote on pages 483-484).

Conclusion

The above documents provide ample proof that the early church preached and believed the doctrine of a literal one thousand year reign of Christ on earth to be shared by the church saints.

With the current doctrinal drift of evangelicalism the doctrine of amillennialism has had something of a renewal. Unlike traditional amillennialism this new movement targets the issue of Israel's place in the end-time. It is largely known as replacement/theology because they claim God is all through with Israel and the many promises of their renewal and recovery belong to the church. This position has no support in church history. It has no support in the present circumstances of Israel. It is the product of revival of the hermeneutics of Origen, one of the later church fathers who taught that scripture should not be taken literally but spiritualized.

In less than a decade the revival of amillennialism has made an impact on the Bible-believing churches. Most people are not aware that this doctrine was born in Roman Catholicism and unfortunately at the time of the reformation it was carried on to Protestantism. During the late reformation years the Pietist and Anabaptist revived the teaching of Pre-millennialism. By the beginning of the 1800's Pre-millennialism was revived in England and Ireland and by 1900 a large majority of evangelicals were Pre-millenarian.

An inductive study of Revelation 20 in its context confirms that the First Century church was right in their expectation of Christ literally reigning on earth for a thousand years after His Second Coming.

Appendix D

Revelation and the Restoration of Israel

The replacement/theology being propagated today cannot be reconciled with the inspired scriptures. This teaching rests on the premise that Israel has no future. They, therefore assume that all the promises of restoration for Israel found in the Old Testament prophets are now to be claimed by the New Testament church. This strange interpretation comes from imposing Origen's hermeneutics on those passages. He denied that any of those passages were to be taken literally and therefore took the liberty to spiritualize the passages.

The spiritualized version is not consistent with history while the literal interpretations are consistent with history. Beginning with the captivity of Judah, Israel was no longer an independent nation. Israel had been under judgment for twenty-five hundred years spiritually blighted, deported from their land and with no independent nation.

The Old Testament prophets never once announce the termination of this covenant people. Instead, they clearly prophesied her spiritual and political recovery in the end of the age. That plan is right on schedule. For more than a century the Jews have been returning to the land. As the prophets indicated they have returned in unbelief.

In May, 1948 the nation of Israel was declared by the United Nations to be a sovereign state and remains so until this day. They have a significant role in international affairs. This little country has a strong economy and is very advanced in the field of technology and in the military. They have been news-worthy most every day of their existence. The incredible thing is that Israel is where she is supposed to be at the beginning of the tribulation period according to the book of Daniel and the book of Revelation. God is obviously working in the circumstances of Israel today and will continue to do so until she is restored both spiritually and politically as called for by the prophets.

It would be helpful to review some of these prophecies that show the wonderful future Israel will enjoy in the last days and on into eternity. From the many passages in the book of Ezekiel we select the following,

> "Then he said unto me, Son of man, these bones are the whole house of Israel, behold they say, our bones are dried, and our hope is lost: and we are cast off from our parts. Therefore prophecy and say unto them, thus saith the Lord God; Behold O my people, I will open your graves and cause you to come up out of your graves, and will bring you into the land of Israel.
>
> And you know that I am the Lord, when I have opened your graves, O my people, and brought you out of your graves.

And shall put my Spirit in you, and you shall live, and I shall place you in your own land: then shall ye know that I the Lord has spoken it, and performed it saith the Lord" (Ezekiel 37:11-14).

In the same chapter Ezekiel predicts their return to the land and the establishment of the nation. Ezekiel continues,

"And say unto them, thus saith the Lord God; Behold I will take the children of Israel from among the heathen, wither they have gone, and will gather them on every side, and bring them into their own land.

I will make them one nation in the land upon the mountains of Israel; and one king shall be king to them all: and they shall be no more two nations, neither shall they be divided into two kingdoms anymore at all" (Ezekiel 37: 21,22).

These prophecies clearly indicate that God has plans for the future of Israel. The complete restoration of Israel awaits the return of Christ. The book of Revelation walks the reader through the tough times of Israel during the tribulation period. We have learned from Daniel 9 that the seventieth week yet to be a part of Israel's history will bring them into a short but very severe time of testing and suffering just prior to Christ's Second Coming.

Jeremiah wrote under the inspiration of the Holy Spirit prophesied also of these end-time dealings with the covenant nation of Israel:

"And this shall be the covenant that I shall make with the house of Israel; after those days, saith the Lord, I will put my law in their inward parts, and write it in their hearts; and will be their God, and they shall be my people and every man his brother, saying know the Lord; for they shall all know Me, from the least of them to the greatest of them, saith the Lord: for I will forgive their iniquity, and I will remember their sins no more.

Thus saith the Lord, which gives the sun for a light by day, and the ordinance of the moon and the stars for a light by night, which divideth the seas when the waves thereof roar; the Lord of hosts is His name.

If those ordinances depart from before me, saith the Lord, then the seed of Israel shall also cease from being a nation before me forever" (Jeremiah 31:34-36).

The above scriptures are only a few of the prophecies of Israel in the end-time. Moses prophesied the same thing as recorded in Deuteronomy just as Israel was about to cross the Jordan.

"Then the Lord thy God will turn thy captivity, and have compassion upon thee, and will return and gather thee from all the nations, whither the Lord thy God hath scattered thee. If any of thine be driven out unto the outmost parts of heaven, form thence will the Lord thy God gather thee, and from thence will he fetch thee.

And the Lord thy God will bring thee into the land which thy fathers possessed, and thou shall possess it; and do thee good, and multiply thee above thy fathers" (Deuteronomy 30:3-5).

That promise was given to Israel more than four thousand years ago and it is beginning to come to pass in the 21st century. What lies ahead can be seen in the references to Israel in the book of Revelation especially from chapter ten to the end of the book. Israel is still on God's agenda.

Appendix E

Revelation and Judgment

The creeds and theological statements of many Protestant churches claim a general judgment of all saints and sinners at the same time. They believe that the Great White Throne judgment described in Revelation 20:11-15 is that general judgment. A careful study of this passage will disprove such a notion.

Those called to this judgment are the "dead." They died in their sins without repenting and accepting Christ's atonement for sin. The books will be opened and they will be judged with fairness. God keeps an accurate record of man's sins and from this record the wicked will be judged.

The book of life will be opened for those who insist they lived a good life and were even religious and insist they should not be judged. Their names will be absent from the book of life for they did not accept Christ as their Savior.

Nothing in this passage suggests that the believers are dead. They have already been resurrected from the dead and lived in the presence of Christ for a full thousand years.

Because they had turned to Christ and been saved from their sins their wickedness was judged at the cross when Christ died for their sins. The saved will have a judgment but it will not determine their eternal destiny. That was accomplished by the death and resurrection of Jesus.

The Bible plainly teaches that the dead in Christ will be resurrected at the rapture and the living Christians will be changed to immortal body and caught up with the resurrected saints to meet the Lord up in the air.

The Apostle Paul speaks twice in his epistles of the judgment seat of Christ. This judgment is for believers and has an entirely different purpose than the Great White Throne judgment. The Judgment Seat of Christ will take place right after the rapture. This judgment will evaluate the life of the believer after they are saved and up until their death. The Lord will carefully observe their deeds and works and failures and determine what rewards they are worthy of. Paul remarks that even though all their works were unacceptable and burned in the fire they themselves will be saved as by fire. To understand the Judgment Seat of Christ, the following scriptures must be considered.

> "For we must all appear before the Judgment Seat of Christ; that everyone may receive the things done in the body, according to what he hath done, whether it be good or bad" (2 Corinthians 5:10).

> "But why doest thou judge thy brother? Or why doest thou set at naught thy brother? For we shall al stand before the Judgment Seat of Christ. For it is written, as I live saith the Lord, every knee shall bow to me, and

every tongue shall confess to God. So then every one of us shall give account of himself to God" (Romans 14:10-12).

The believer does well to keep close accounts with God and with a pure heart seek always to do His will. For rich blessing and eternal rewards await those who follow Him faithfully.

These scriptures make it clear the believers will not be brought under judgment at the Great White Throne. However, they will be present not to be judged but to be judges. Some astounding truths are brought out in the sixth chapter of I Corinthians. Paul was rebuking the believers in this congregation for failing to judge among themselves disputes over earthly things. Paul said,

"Do you not know that the saints will judge the world? And if the world shall be judged by you, are ye unworthy to judge the smallest matter?

Know ye not that we shall judge angels? How more things that pertain to this life" (I Corinthians 6:2,3).

The saints (the believers) are destined to reign with Christ and also to judge with Him. At that awful judgment at the Great White Throne, the saints will judge with the Lord Jesus Christ.

It cannot be rightly said that the Great White Throne is a general judgment. The wicket only will come under judgment in that day. No doubt the fallen angels will be judged then as well. At least on this occasion the redeemed will judge the worldly and angels as the scripture says.

The teachings of the scriptures are that separate judgments will be carried out for believers and non-believers. Revelation 20 shows they will take place a thousand years apart and will have radically different objectives. The judgment seat of Christ will judge the lives of the saints and reward them accordingly. The Great White Throne is a judgment of eternal damnation.

At the appearance of the Great White Throne the scripture says, "From whose face the earth and the heaven fled away; and there was found no place for them" (Revelation 20:11).

This judgment and the end of the heavens and the earth took place simultaneously.

At that moment the Apostle John who witnessed these visions and wrote them down for us cried out, "And I saw a new heaven and a new earth; for the first heaven and the first earth were passed away; and there was no more sea" (Revelation 21:1). At this point not only history but time is terminated and eternity has taken over.

Bibliography

Alford, Dean Henry, Greek New Testament Volume IV, Cambridge: Deighton, Bell and Company, 1871

Bengal, John A., Gnoman of the Greek New Testament Volume V, Edinburgh: T. and T. Clarke,
First published in 1742

Blackstone, W.E. Jesus is Coming, New York: Fleming H. Revell Company, 1898

Fruchtenbaum, Arnold G,. The Footsteps of the Messiah, Tustin, CA: Ariel Ministries, 2004

Gaebelein, Arno C., The Revelation, New York: Our Hope, 1915

Grant, F.W., The Prophetic History of the Church, New York: Loizeauz, 1902

Hamilton, Gavin, Coming Kingdom Glories. McCall Baber, 1965

Hamilton, Gavin, Maranatha, McCall Baber, No Date

Hoyt, Herman, Studies in Revelation, Winona Lake, IN: BMH Books, 1977

Ironside, H.A., <u>Lectures on the Book of Revelation</u>, Neptune, NJ: Loizeaux, 1979

Larkin, Clarence, <u>The Book of Revelation</u>, Glenside, PA: Clarence Larkin Estate, 1919

Marsh, F.E., <u>Advent Addresses</u>, Salem, OH: Convention Book Store, No Date

McClain, Alva J., <u>Daniel's Prophecy of the Seventy Weeks</u>, Winona Lake, IN: BMH Books, 2007

Newell, William, <u>The Book of Revelation</u>, Chicago, IL: Moody Press, 1935

Pettingil, William L., <u>Simple Studies in the Book of Revelation</u>, Philadelphia, PA: Philadelphia School of the Bible

Phillips, John, <u>Exporing the Revelation</u>, Grand Rapids: Kregle Publications, No Date

Scott, Walter, <u>Exposition of the Revelation of Jesus Christ</u>, Westwood, NJ: Fleming Revel, No Date

Seiss, J.A., The Apocalypse, Volumes I, II, III, New York: Charles C. Cook, 1917

Seiss, J.A., The Last Times, Louisville, KY: Pentecostal Publishing Company, 1878

Simpson, A.B., <u>Back to Patmos</u>, New York: Christian Alliance Publishing Company, 1914

Stevens, W.C., <u>Revelation the Crown Jewel of the Prophecy</u>, Harrisburg, PA: Christian Alliance Publishing Company, 1928

Tatford, Frederick K., <u>Daniel and His Prophecy</u>, Klock and Klock, 1980 reprint

Telfer, John, <u>The Coming Kingdom of God</u>, London: Marshall Brothers, No Date

Tozer, A.W., <u>Jesus is Victor</u>, Camp Hill, PA: Zur Publishing, 1984

Walvoord, John and Zuck, Roy, <u>The Bible Knowledge Commentary of the New Testament</u>, Wheaton, IL: Victor Books, 1985

Index

A
Abraham 41, 107, 108
Abomination of Desolation 67
Alford, Dean 72, 90
Alpha and Omega 4
Amillenialism 140
Anabaptist 14
Ancient of Days 5
Antichrist 67, 68, 73, 77, 79, 83, 85, 91, 92
Apostasy 18, 19, 20
Apostolic Age 10
Ark of the Covenant 61
Armageddon 64, 74, 75, 77, 79, 84, 96
Artaxerxes 33
Asia Minor 7, 9
Authority of Scripture 18

B
Babylon 82, 83, 85, 90, 91
Barnabas 138
Beast 65, 67, 68, 73
Biblical Numerics 10
Black Horse 35
Bottomless Pit 49
Brethren 14
Bride of Christ 101, 102, 107

C
Calvin, John 14
Church Age 18, 20, 21, 23
Clarke, Adam 5
Crowned Christ 2, 4

D
Daniel 32, 33, 34, 41
Demonic Locusts 49, 50
Dragon 62, 63, 66, 67

E
Earth-Dwellers 78, 88, 89
Earthquakes 36, 60, 81, 82, 83, 84
Enoch 96, 100
Eternal Age 110
Ephesus 11
Euphrates River 50
Eusebius 139, 140

F
False Prophet 67, 68
Fifth Trumpet 48
First Bowl of Wrath 78
First Love 11
First Seal 34
First Trumpet 46
Fourth Bowl of Wrath 79

G
Gaebelein, A.C 156
Garden of Eden 111
German Higher Criticism 16
Great Tribulation 16, 18, 31, 32, 33, 69, 75, 89
Great White Throne 103, 149, 151, 152

H
Higher Life Movement 15

I
Ireneas 139
Israel 32, 144, 146, 147

J
John 6, 7, 23, 24, 25, 89, 105, 106, 107

K
Kelly, William 83
Kings and Priests 2, 100
King of Kings 125

L
Laodicea 16
Lake of Fire and Brimstone
Lamb of God 26, 27, 28, 29, 40
Liberal Modernism 17
Lion of Tribe of Judea 26
Literal Interpretation 128
Little Book 53, 55
Living Creations 25, 27
Love Feast 94

M
Man Child 62
Marriage Supper of the Lamb 94, 95
Martyr, Justin 139
Megiddo 96
Mennonites 14
Middle East 18, 79
Mid-Tribulation Rapture 133
Millennial Reign 60, 95, 98, 99, 100, 128
Moravians 14
Mount of Olives 83, 84, 99
Mount Zion 71, 72, 107
Mystery, Babylon Mother of Harlots 86

N
New Earth 105, 106
Newell, William R 58
New Jerusalem 106, 107, 108

New Testament Church 17, 28
O
Old Testament Saints 28
One Thousand Years
Origen 140, 143
P
Pale Horse 36
Palestine 88
Papias 138
Patmos 4, 8, 18
Pentecost 10, 11
Pentecost, J. Dwight 110
Pergomas 12
Peters, George M.H 140
Philadelphia 15
Polycarp 138, 139
Post-Tribulation Rapture 133
Pre-Millennialism 138, 141
Pre-Tribulation Rapture 133
Pre-Wrath Rapture 133
R
Rapture 21, 28, 131, 132, 133, 134
Received Text 28
Red Horse 35
Restoration of Israel 143 145, 146, 147
Revived Roman Empire . 65, 66, 69, 88, 90
Roman Catholic 12
Roman Empire 66
S
Sardis ..14
Scarlet Woman 86, 87
Scott, Walter 90

Sealed 144,000 Jews 40, 41, 42, 59, 71, 72
Second Bowl of Wrath 78
Second Coming of Christ 16, 31, 72, 132, 137
Second Trumpet 47
Seven Golden Candlesticks 5
Seven Stars 7
Seven Bowls of Wrath 77, 79
Seventy Weeks of Daniel 33, 34
Simpson, A.B 116
Sixth Bowl of Wrath 79
Smyrna 11
Stephanos 25
T
The Sealed Book 26, 27, 34, 35, 36, 37
The Throne Room 24, 25
The Title Deed 26
The Twenty-Four Elders 27, 28, 29
Thunder and Lightning 25
Thyratira 13
Times of the Gentiles 58, 61, 66
Tozer, A.W 50, 51
Tree of Life 111, 112, 113
Two Witnesses 58, 59, 60
W
Waldensians 14
Wescott and Hort Text 28, 29
Wesleyan Revival 15
Whitefield Revival 15

Z

Zechariah 80, 81, 83
Zionism 58
Zwingli, Ulric 14

Made in the USA
Charleston, SC
27 March 2013